POTAGER

to Paula

I hope you enjoy these recipes —

POTAGER

FRESH GARDEN COOKING
IN THE FRENCH STYLE

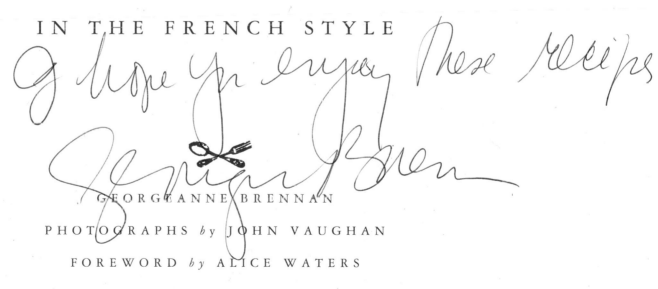

Georgeanne Brennan

GEORGEANNE BRENNAN

PHOTOGRAPHS *by* JOHN VAUGHAN

FOREWORD *by* ALICE WATERS

CHRONICLE BOOKS

SAN FRANCISCO

Brennan, Georgeanne, 1943–
Potager : fresh garden cooking in the French style /
by Georgeanne Brennan ; photography by John Vaughan
p. cm.   Includes index.
ISBN 0-8118-3041-1 (pb.)
1. Cookery (vegetables) 2. Cookery (fruit)
1. Title. TX801.B6953 1992
641.6'5—dc20

Printed in Hong Kong.

Distributed in Canada by Raincoast Books
9050 Shaughnessy Street
Vancouver, B.C. V6P 6E5
10 9 8 7 6 5

Chronicle Books LLC
85 Second Street
San Francisco, CA 94105

www.chroniclebooks.com

Deep-Dish Black Cabbage and Bean Soup with Anchovy Crust (page 118)

THE

POTAGER

COOKBOOK

TABLE OF CONTENTS

FOREWORD

by Alice Waters

It has been more than twenty years since my friends and I started Chez Panisse. From the very start we had a vision of freshness that drove us beyond the conventional American sources of foodstuffs of those days, the supermarkets and the big wholesale produce brokers. We knew, from books and from our experiences abroad, that there could be a variety and immediacy to our menus that could transform our cooking into something alive and new to most of our customers. So we scavenged wild greens from vacant lots and plucked watercress from roadside creeks. We snuck down the neighbors' driveways and snipped rosemary from their hedges and took nasturtiums from their borders. And we searched—all too often in vain—for farmers and gardeners who were growing the cornucopia of choices we knew from the country markets and gardens of France described so lovingly by Elizabeth David and Richard Olney.

For in those days even the seeds for so many of the vegetables and herbs we craved were unavailable. American seed catalogs were dominated by varieties seemingly bred mainly for looks and size. Georgeanne Brennan helped change all this. Thanks to her seed company, Le Marché, and others like it, it is possible again to plant and grow and harvest a wonderful range of greens, roots, tubers, and fruits. This is the variety that our ancestors knew so well before home economists, agribusinessmen and creeping standardization of taste began to drive us out of our gardens and suppress the seasons. After a generation or two of blandness, uniformity, and the year-round availability of relatively few kinds of vegetables, many of us were primed for fresh flavor, variety, and seasonality in our kitchens. Gradually this vision is becoming a reality. Community garden projects and private gardens proliferate and farmers' markets flourish across the country.

How can you convey, in words and pictures in a cookbook, what it is to pick something at its peak of ripeness from your own garden, and cook it and eat it, and how different that is from cooking and eating something processed and packaged from the supermarket? How can you get across that sense of immediacy? Georgeanne Brennan's book effectively demonstrates, through recipes and photographs, just how thrilling it can be to cook, in seasons, food straight from the garden, knowing exactly the where and when of what you're eating.

What are the pleasures of a *potager*? I can never go to the garden in my backyard without a sense of what a privilege it is to be able to grow at least some of my own food. What immense satisfaction in knowing that we are part of the endless procession of the seasons. By making compost out of my kitchen scraps and returning it to the land to nourish new growth, I join in the natural cycle of rebirth, while wasting nothing and supporting the health of the bigger ecosystem. A kitchen garden also brings built-in variation to your cooking. Without even having to think about it, you'll learn what it is to cook things as they grow and change in their own life cycles, from early in their season to late: to know,

for example, what it is to eat little fava beans picked just shy of maturity and sprinkled raw on salad; and then to eat them slightly sautéed in olive oil when they have reached their prime of tenderness and flavor; and finally, when all you have are the tough ones that are starting to dry out, to make a purée of them with rosemary and garlic. You learn the subtleties of ripeness almost by osmosis.

The choice of recipes in this volume is appropriate to its subject. These are recipes that don't embellish or disguise their ingredients: they treat them for what they are and preserve their home-grown integrity. These are inspired dishes that conjure up the seasonal mood of the table and the aesthetic of honest simplicity. There are fragrant stews and savory puddings, the enticing flavors of bitter along with the sweet.

John Vaughan's photos are particularly beautiful because this is real food from real gardens, photographed in natural light. In fact, this entire book, pictures and recipes, strikes me as having been composed under natural light. It is clear-headed and modest and down-to-earth. This book celebrates the best-tasting and least expensive food and will surely convince you of the timeliness and wisdom of the words of old Voltaire: "We must cultivate our garden!"

INTRODUCTION

Red and Yellow Tomato Platter with Balsamic Vinegar (page 55)

INTRODUCTION

*otager* cooking and its counterpart, *cuisine de marché*, are based on the use of fresh, seasonal ingredients. For centuries the French have had *potagers*, or "kitchen gardens," and open markets as sources of fresh fruits and vegetables. French cooks, no matter how humble or how exalted, rely on daily access to just harvested, flavorful ingredients from their home gardens or from market growers' gardens no more than a half day distant. Even though today supermarkets of every size abound in France, and it is possible to buy anything either frozen or plastic-wrapped and shipped from another continent, the *potager* and market traditions remain strong.

In recent years the United States has enjoyed a renaissance in kitchen gardening and in open-air farmers' markets, urban green markets, and specialty groceries and supermarket produce departments selling regional fruits and vegetables. For the first time in decades, a majority of American cooks have access to the same fine-quality seasonal ingredients that French cooks have always taken for granted. Much of the French reputation for wonderful food is founded on the ongoing traditions of *cuisine de potager* and *cuisine de marché*, in which the best ingredients are chosen for the preparation of every dish. These are not necessarily the most expensive ingredients, but they are always the freshest, most seasonal ones.

Over the years in France, I have often lingered with family and friends over a simple seasonal meal of summer tomatoes liberally dressed with a fruity olive oil vinaigrette and fresh basil, *les omelettes aux fines herbes*, and aromatic Charentais melons. On a chilly night in fall, we might dine on a rich beef daube, a sturdy *mesclun* salad, and, for dessert, a warm persimmon flan. A composed salad of Belgian endive and citrus is a common beginning for a winter meal, followed by plump roast chickens and winter roots. In springtime salads are made with new potatoes and tiny peas and seasoned with mint. They accompany thick chops grilled with fresh spring herbs, and dessert is an irresistible cherry tart.

For me, the best meals are the simplest ones, made with seasonal ingredients and presented in a thoughtful, personal way. Time after time, sitting at the table in the home of French friends, I am struck by the sense that there is no occasion more important than the basic act of breaking bread with friends and family.

The French have two wonderful sources for seasonal produce, the gardens of *les maraîchers* and their own *potagers*. *Le maraîcher*, or "the market gardener," brings the products of his commercial garden, often comprising only a few acres, to one of several different types of open markets where people come to buy direct from the producer or his distributor.

The *potager*, which comes from the French word *potage*, or "soup," is a kitchen garden that provides the daily seasonal vegetables, berries, and cutting flowers for the family. A few fruit trees, if space allows, are planted at the edge of the plot. Traditionally, every French household from château to cottage has a *potager*, and although these gardens are beginning to disappear in some areas of France, there are still enough of them throughout the country to convince me that the kitchen garden tradition is healthy and viable.

Sometimes the *potager* is very small, perhaps only a ten-foot-square plot. Despite its size, it will be brimming with peas and carrots, and strawberry plants will line its edges. Herbs will be tucked into any bare spot, along with a potato plant or two. A single cherry or pear tree may stand at its edge.

I love looking at these gardens. No cultural rules seem to be in force about size or location. Sometimes the beans, peppers, eggplants, and tomatoes are planted right in front of the house; other times they are planted along the driveway or a walkway. *Potagers* are intensely personal. Their owners embellish them with an eclectic mix of flowers, shrubs, and vines. Stone, tile, and brick walls, stepping stones, decorated cement tables, cheerfully painted tool sheds, miscellaneous overstuffed armchairs, and highly individualistic scarecrows are some of the other accoutrements of a large French *potager*.

My first *potager* was planted not in France, but in a bedroom community in northern California. I had recently returned there with my family after living for several years in the French countryside, where neighbors gave me fruits and vegetables from their gardens and I went shopping almost daily at open markets. Back in California, I was desperate for the taste of the fresh seasonal foods that I had become accustomed to using in the kitchen.

The backyard of our house was too shady for a garden, and besides the children didn't want their play space taken up with tomatoes and beans. The front yard, however, was wonderfully sunny and the soil seemed nice and rich, so we dug up half the lawn that had been planted there by the previous owner and put in our garden.

We filled the place to overflowing with French melon and cornichon cucumber vines, *haricot vert* plants, wild borders of zinnias and cosmos, towering pillars of red Marmande tomatoes, bushes of yellow pear and yellow plum tomatoes, several prolific zucchini plants and masses of herbs. Most of our garden was grown from seeds French friends sent to us.

All summer long strangers would stop to admire our *potager* and we feasted on its bounty nightly. Every morning I went out into the garden to see which melons might be ripe for dinner and which ones might be ready to eat the next day, to pick beans and tomatoes, and to pull back the cucumber vines to look for

carrots line beds of precision-planted lettuces, which are replaced in summer by equally elegant patterns of tomato bushes and *haricot* vines. Or it can be as random as the Michauds' *potager* in the Berry, not far from the Loire River.

In the garden of the Michauds, lettuces stand side-by-side with pansies, peek out from under the leaves of artichoke plants, and also grow in proper rows. Tomatoes climb alongside huge flowering poppies, and potatoes are right at home with peonies. "Everything has a right to try to live, once it is started," says Mme. Michaud. "If I find a flower seed has fallen and taken root by chance, I find a place in my garden to plant it where it will have room to grow."

Although almost any French household with access to a patch of ground and some water will maintain a basic *potager* of leeks, peas, carrots, lettuces, and herbs, another source for fresh ingredients is the wonderful open markets that abound in every city and tiny village. The markets are collections of individual stalls or stands, each occupied by someone specializing in a single category of food. Vegetable and fruit stalls are next to the poultry stand, which is near the butcher, who borders the olive vendor, and so on.

Essentially there are three types of open markets: fixed markets, open daily, with hundreds of permanent stalls built inside a covered market hall; market streets where shop owners set up stands on the sidewalk in front of their stores; and, finally, roving markets. Unlike the covered markets and the market streets, which are found only in the larger cities, the roving markets are everywhere. They are held mornings on the same day each week in towns, villages, and cities throughout France. The location never varies from one market day to the next, year in and year out. Most often

their tiny cornichons. Finally, I would pick an armload of flowers and carry it into the house. Some days I chose flowers in all shades of red, other days only yellows and oranges, depending upon my mood. I loved the daily ritual that I was discovering, and today that same morning garden tour and gathering is an integral part of my life.

The *potager* is not like the gardens of our American forebears, filled with hundreds of pounds of fruits and vegetables to be "put up" for the winter. The purpose of the *potager* is to provide a harvest of vegetables, flowers, and berries that can be enjoyed that same day. The design can be as elaborate and as geometrical as the Potager du Roy, the splendid vegetable garden at Versailles. There, in spring, perfect rows of leeks and

the market is located in the town's main square and radiates out along the nearby streets.

Market vendors come with their wares early in the morning, arriving in a collection of colorful vehicles. Specialized market vans have awnings and tables that fold out from sliding side panels. Other vans have built-in shelves to accommodate boxes of fruits and vegetables. Tiny Renaults and Peugeots, with miniscule cabs and oversized backs, arrive bulging with wooden boxes and cardboard cartons full of fresh produce. Perfectly built for navigating narrow streets, these sturdy vehicles carry more crates tied precariously on the overhead racks. Vintage cars, such as low-slung black Citroëns, still make an occasional appearance at the markets. When the cavernous trunk is opened, it usually reveals something exotic, such as baskets of freshly gathered chanterelle mushrooms or a pound or two of black truffles.

My favorite market vehicles are the bicycles. I love to watch people pedaling up to their assigned places in the market, then propping up their bicycles and undoing the bungee cords holding baskets firmly to the handlebars and the rack behind the seat. Once they have carefully unloaded neatly tied bundles of fresh bouquets garnis or branches of sweet-smelling bay from the baskets, they arrange their wares precisely on a small cloth or blanket on the ground in front of them.

The bicycle vendors sell out quickly it seems, because they are the first to leave the market, pedaling off shortly before noon. By one thirty all of the other vendors are gone and the square and the streets are empty. The market, so tightly jammed earlier with shoppers and wares, now seems as if it had been a mirage.

The market growers themselves are most often the vendors at the roving markets, and when you buy a head of lettuce or a kilo or two of potatoes, you are probably buying it from the market grower himself, or a member of his extended family who actually prepared the soil, planted the seed, and nurtured it to maturity. Living and cultivating their plots no more than a half day distant, market growers make weekly rounds of the open markets, "roving" from one to another. Of course, a hundred years ago, a "half day distant" was deter-

mined by horsecart and usually measured no more than twenty miles. Today the distance has grown to as much as two hundred miles, but other than distance and type of vehicle, very little has changed about these markets. The personal relationship between the grower and the customer is still intense. Located year after year in the same spot in the market, the grower is a reliable, companionable source of fresh, seasonal food.

Over the years I have periodically helped my French neighbor sell her summer melons in the local open markets. Years ago, when my husband and I first bought our house—a mass of tumbling sixteenth-century stone without electricity or running water—in the back country of Provence, the neighboring building was occupied by the Luchesis, grape farmers and market growers. We became fast friends. Our children played dress-up and hide-and-seek together and Françoise and I chatted as we did our laundry, washing out overalls and diapers in the huge tubs next to the well. We pumped the water into the tubs by turning the handle on a big iron wheel. She and Maurice shared their *potager* with us, insisting, "Treat it like it's yours. Take what you want. There's plenty." It was from Françoise and my other neighbor, Victorine Frenet, that I learned about cooking from the garden. So when Françoise asked me if I wanted to go to the nearby open markets with her to help her sell the melons she and her husband grew, it seemed natural to say yes.

I drove the Luchesis' little Renault van. At the market, Françoise and I would unload several hundred pounds of melons. She didn't use a table; we just stacked the boxes of melons in front of us. At first, Françoise did most of the talking and selling, while I handled the scale and the money. After a few trips I began to learn, under Françoise's tutelage, to distin-

guish a perfectly ripe Canary melon, one that would be at its peak of flavor in time for that day's lunch, from one that would reach its peak the next day. The ability to tell fine degrees of ripeness was necessary for two reasons. First, customers didn't just ask for a melon. They specified a melon that would be perfectly ripe for a particular meal. Secondly, if you sold a melon that was not just right, you would hear about it the next market day, and such a mistake made too often would result in the loss of customers.

I still go to those same markets once in a while with Françoise, and standing in the same spot on the same town square where we first stood eighteen years ago, customers coming to buy a melon or two will remember me from years past. We exchange inquiries about one another's children and families, and comment on the weather and maybe, in the right mood, a little local politics.

I like the characteristic sense of continuity and permanence of these roving markets. Every summer I can go to the Sunday morning market in Salernes and buy a plump chicken or rabbit from Marie-Pierre, the poultry vendor. At the same market I can purchase my potted geraniums for the season from the man with the blue beret. I've never learned his name, but it doesn't matter because he is always there.

In the covered markets and in the stalls lining the market streets, the continuity is similar to that of the roving markets. The shoppers have their favorite vendors and they have done business together over the years. The one notable difference that does exist among the markets is that the competition seems to be fiercer in the covered markets and on the market streets, and so vendors will go to great lengths to erect displays that are nothing less than works of art. Four-foot-high

mounds of brilliant white-tipped red radishes rise next to staggering pyramids of Brittany artichokes. Smooth, pink pigs' heads top terrines of *rillettes* and pâté, and in winter whole wild boars are triumphantly displayed, decked out with red ribbons and sprays of green pine. The sights are truly splendid, and, as one might imagine, the taste and quality had better live up to the displays. Such concern is not only a matter of pride, but of commercial survival.

Although kiwifruits, bananas, and other tropical imports can be found almost anytime of the year, seasonal produce dominates the open market just as it does the home garden. The season can be as readily identified by walking along the market stalls as it can by looking in kitchen plots. Heaps of asparagus, artichokes, strawberries, peas, and fava beans are the clues to spring. Tomatoes, eggplants, thick, meaty peppers, and all kinds of beans and melons fill the stalls in summer. In fall late pears, apples, and quinces appear, along with the beautiful deep red and buff French pumpkin varieties. Winter displays are dominated by cold-hardy cabbages and kale, by root vegetables, and by forced vegetables such as Belgian endive.

French cooks, like their American counterparts, are not limited to seasonality, of course, thanks to refrigeration, freezing, and long-distance shipping. *Cuisine de marché* and *cuisine de potager*, however, remain the mainstays of the best French cooking. Adherents of these venerable traditions staunchly maintain that what is in season is best in terms of quality, abundance, price, and, ultimately, taste.

Cuisine de marché and *potager* cooking are finding enthusiasts in the United States. Drawing partly on our own agricultural traditions and partly on our love of the culinary styles of other countries such as France, two

drive of their customers. Their tomatoes come to market like French ones—truly ripened on the vine. Field-cut cabbage, small, purple-topped turnips, dozens of apple varieties, pears, and peaches exhibit the same quality, diversity, and taste that is associated with seasonal food in France. Some of their customers are restaurants; others are specialty produce markets or produce departments of large supermarket chains. A very important segment of their clientele, however, is made up of people who come to buy at the rapidly growing number of local farmers' and green markets. These shoppers are not in search of bargains, but of quality and variety. The old farmer-to-cook tradition is being reborn in the United States.

American cooks today, unlike fifteen years ago when, in desperation, I planted my first *potager*, have sources of fine-quality fresh fruits, vegetables, and herbs through farmers' markets, specialty markets, and some supermarket produce sections. In fall a trip to a farmers' market will no doubt turn up knobby quinces, a choice of apples, fragrant late-summer pears, and perhaps some plump leeks and the first of the season's hard squashes. Poach the fruit in wine or make a tart. Use the leeks in combination with cod to prepare a bubbling, crispy gratin, and turn the squashes into a substantial soup. *Voilà—cuisine de marché.*

Cuisine de marché takes no space and less planning and time than planting and maintaining a *potager*. But I have come to love *potager* cooking and that is what I have tried to re-create at home in California. My garden—often ragged-looking, sometimes pristinely manicured—always provides me with something to cook and flowers for my table. Should my garden fail me, though, I too, like the French, can now go to a market and buy seasonal fruits and vegetables.

phenomena are occurring. People who have never planted a seed or dug a hole for a tree are ordering French lettuce seeds through mail-order catalogs and haunting the aisles of garden centers, wondering if they really could grow yellow tomatoes. First-time gardeners are creating individualized *potagers* of vegetables and flowers, and finding the experience exciting and rewarding, just as I did with my first *potager*.

The second phenomenon is the increasing number of a new breed of American market growers. Like the French growers, they live within a half day's

SPRING

Grilled Pork Chops with Mint Soufflé (page 42)

SPRING

The Season of New Growth

he lengthening days and rising temperatures of spring provide the necessary conditions for germination and growth. The traditional spring vegetables are harvested early in the season: new leafy greens, the first stalks and buds, small roots and tubers, and immature seeds in tender pods. The year's first stone fruits and soft fruits appear.

Cuisine de potager and *cuisine de marché* are in all their glory in springtime. Market stalls are bursting with spring vegetables and fruits and the kitchen garden is flush with new growth of every kind. A single foray for greens is likely to produce tiny green and red butter, Batavia, romaine, and looseleaf lettuces; delicate *mâche*; young arugula; spinach; chives; sorrel; and mint. Fat asparagus stalks, slim leeks, green garlic, and onions are ready to pick; so are budding artichokes and the year's first plump, red strawberries. Radish and carrot roots pull up easily from the loose earth, and new potatoes can be dug with a single thrust and turn of the shovel.

Fava bean and pea plants dangle green pods that quickly swell with soft, green seeds, and cherry clusters begin to ripen on the trees.

Daily shopping at the open markets offers the French cook the same fruits and vegetables picked from a *potager,* as well as the wild mushrooms, stalks, and greens that are an integral part of Gallic spring cooking. When possible, though, the French prefer to gather wild edibles rather than buy them from the market vendors. For a few short weeks in spring, people of all ages fan out across the countryside where wild greens and stalks flourish in ploughed fields and along roadsides. They avidly harvest sharp-tasting dandelions and resinous-flavored wild mustard greens before they become too strong and stringy to eat. Wild asparagus, leeks, and morel mushrooms are hunted with even greater enthusiasm, although for the uninitiated they are more difficult to find than the wild greens.

Spring salads, whether the ingredients are garden grown, gathered wild, or purchased at the market, are as varied as the season itself. They may consist of one variety of greens, such as dandelion, or of a mixture. A spring salad will also often showcase a single seasonal vegetable, such as asparagus simply dressed with a good olive oil. The flavors of spring greens range from the mild, nutty taste of *mâche* to the intense, strong bite of wild dandelions, and allow for all sorts of taste variations in between, both singly and in combination. *Mesclun*, the Provençal mixture of greens of varying shape, texture, and taste, sports its wildest combinations this time of the year.

Spring's fresh salad ingredients are easily turned into soups and stews. Because they are early growth and quite tender, the greens need little cooking. They are quickly wilted in broth to make rustic soups or used as fillings in elegant galantines. Peas, favas, and asparagus take only moments of cooking before they can be tossed into pastas or folded into savory puddings or soufflés. Even vegetable stews of artichoke hearts and fava beans need only brief cooking.

It is difficult to do any cooking at all with the first fruits of spring because they taste so good eaten raw. Lingering over a bowl of cherries or strawberries, savoring them one by one, is as pleasant a way to finish a meal as one could wish. After the season has been underway for a few weeks, however, and one has eaten a surfeit of fresh fruits, simply prepared desserts become acceptable. Strawberries marinated in red wine with a little sugar and mint are always welcome, and so are delicate cherry tarts. A final spring preparation for me is putting up a few jars of cherries packed in the strong-flavored Armagnac that I like so well, to store for winter desserts when *les cerises* are long out of season.

Early growth is the foundation of the seasonal table. Everywhere in the *potager* something is growing, ready to be picked for the kitchen, and the open markets are crowded with lush vegetables and fruits. Traditional winter cooking, with its reliance on stored and preserved foods, lies a long time off.

SALAD OF NEW POTATOES, PEAS, AND MINT

Explosive flavor abounds in this simple salad. A bouquet of spring mint is combined with raspberry vinegar and olive oil to coat warm new potatoes and peas. More mint added just before serving enhances the vinegar-infused mint of the dressing.

Ingredients for Salad of New Potatoes, Peas, and Mint

Dressing
1/4 CUP OLIVE OIL
1/4 CUP RASPBERRY VINEGAR
1/4 TEASPOON SALT
1/4 CUP CHOPPED FRESH MINT

12 SMALL NEW POTATOES
1 CUP SHELLED PEAS
1/2 CUP CHICKEN STOCK
8 TO 12 LEAVES BUTTER LETTUCE
1/4 CUP CHOPPED FRESH MINT
FRESH MINT SPRIGS FOR GARNISH

To make the dressing, combine the olive oil, vinegar, salt, and mint in a small bowl. Stir and let stand at room temperature.

Meanwhile, boil the potatoes in water to cover until tender when pierced with a fork, about 20 minutes. Drain and place in a large salad bowl.

While the potatoes are cooking, combine the peas and chicken stock in a small pan. Bring to a boil and boil until the peas are tender. This will take 10 to 20 minutes, depending upon the size and maturity of the peas. If possible, use small, young peas. Drain the peas and add them to the bowl with the potatoes.

Pour the dressing over the peas and potatoes and let stand for 10 to 15 minutes, turning often.

Line individual salad plates with the lettuce leaves. Mound equal amounts of the dressed peas and potatoes on the lettuce. Sprinkle each salad with some of the chopped mint and garnish with a mint sprig. Serve at room temperature.

Serves 3 or 4

LEEKS IN VINAIGRETTE

This is a very simple first course or side dish, but the fine flavor of warm leeks bathed in olive oil and red wine vinegar seems special. If you are growing your own leeks, harvest them when they are quite young, only about half an inch in diameter. They have the most delicate texture at this stage. Otherwise, choose the smallest leeks you can find, or quarter large leeks lengthwise.

20 SMALL, 12 MEDIUM, OR 4 LARGE LEEKS

Dressing
1/2 CUP OLIVE OIL
2 TABLESPOONS DIJON-STYLE OR SIMILAR
        MUSTARD
1/4 CUP RED WINE VINEGAR
1/4 TEASPOON SALT

1/4 TEASPOON FRESHLY GROUND BLACK PEPPER

2 SHALLOTS, FINELY CHOPPED

1 TABLESPOON CHOPPED FRESH PARSLEY FOR
    GARNISH

Trim the root ends from the leeks, leaving the bases intact. Trim the tops of the leeks to a uniform length. If you are using very young leeks, the green tops are nice and tender and only 1 inch need be trimmed. The upper greens of mature leeks tend to be tough and stringy, and all but 2 or 3 inches should be removed.

Place the leeks on a steamer rack and set over gently boiling water. Cover and steam the leeks until ten-der, about 10 minutes for young leeks, and up to 20 min-utes for medium-sized leeks and quartered large leeks.

While the leeks are steaming, make the dress-ing. Place the olive oil is a small bowl. Add the mustard and beat together until the oil thickens. Add the vinegar, salt, pepper, and shallots. Set aside.

Arrange the warm leeks on a serving platter. Pour the dressing over them and turn them gently to coat evenly. Sprinkle with the parsley.

I like the leeks best when they are served slightly warm or at room temperature, but they may also be made ahead and served chilled.

Serves 4

Dandelion Salad with Anchovy Dressing

DANDELION SALAD WITH ANCHOVY DRESSING

The assertive tastes that characterize this salad recall fall and winter foods. Salty, oil-rich anchovies are mashed with garlic and olive oil to form a thick dressing that makes a perfect complement to the rough, strong flavor of wild dandelion greens. A tamer dandelion salad uses bacon, chopped hard-cooked eggs, and green onions, but as a lover of both anchovies and garlic, this is the version I prefer.

1/2 CUP SAVORY CROUTONS (*following recipe*)

Dressing
6 FLAT ANCHOVY FILLETS IN OIL, DRAINED
2 CLOVES GARLIC
1/4 CUP OLIVE OIL
1/2 TEASPOON FRESHLY GROUND BLACK PEPPER

2 BUNCHES DANDELION GREENS

Prepare the croutons and set aside.

To make the dressing, in the bottom of a salad bowl, mash the anchovies and garlic together with the back of a fork or wooden spoon. Gradually stir in the olive oil, then add the black pepper. Set aside.

Trim any thick, woody stem ends off the dandelion greens, leaving only the tender leaves. If the leaves are large, cut them on a long diagonal, into 2 or 3 pieces. Each piece should show some of the deeply serrated leaf edge that is the hallmark of dandelion greens. Leave small leaves whole. You should have about 3 cups leaves. Add the greens to the salad bowl. Toss them with the anchovy dressing until they are thoroughly coated.

Scatter the croutons over the top of the salad and serve.

Serves 4 to 6

SAVORY CROUTONS

------

8 SLICES DRY FRENCH BREAD (1 INCH THICK)
1/4 CUP OLIVE OIL
2 CLOVES GARLIC
1/2 TEASPOON SALT
3 TABLESPOONS MINCED MIXED FRESH HERBS, SUCH AS OREGANO, THYME, AND ROSEMARY

Without removing the crusts, cut the bread into 1-inch cubes. Do not worry if the cubes are not perfectly square. One of their charms is their irregular home made look. Heat the olive oil in a frying pan over medium heat. Add the garlic, reduce the heat to low, and sauté the garlic for 2 or 3 minutes. Add the bread cubes and cook slowly over low heat until golden and crusty, about 4 or 5 minutes on each side.

When done, sprinkle the cubes with the salt and herbs, turn a few times in the pan, and then remove to a paper towel to drain and cool. The croutons may be stored for several days in a closed paper bag.

Makes approximately 32 croutons, about 4 cups

SOUP OF WILD GREENS
WITH *GNOCCHI* AND PROSCIUTTO

In medieval times, dandelion, wild mustard, sorrel, arugula, nettles, and numerous other greens fell into the category known as potherbs—literally, any green that could be cooked and eaten. For the French, gathering wild greens during the spring is a national pastime and the harvest is treated with great respect.

This soup, enriched with plump dumplings and prosciutto, is made with wild greens, but it is equally good prepared with cultivated greens such as spinach, escarole, and chard. My neighbor in Provence, Françoise Luchesi, taught me how to make *gnocchi*. I often whipped up a batch because it was so difficult to find fresh pasta. Now I can find them fresh in so many shops that I seldom make them.

2 POUNDS MIXED GREENS, SUCH AS DANDELION,
    MUSTARD, ARUGULA, SPINACH, AND ESCAROLE
1 TEASPOON OLIVE OIL
1/4 CUP CHOPPED ONION
1/4 CUP CHOPPED FRESH CHIVES
2 CUPS CHICKEN STOCK
1/4 TEASPOON SALT
1/2 POUND FRESH *GNOCCHI*, OR 1/4 CUP
    DRIED *GNOCCHI*
2 OUNCES THINLY SLICED PROSCIUTTO,
    CHOPPED
FRESHLY GRATED ROMANO CHEESE

Thoroughly rinse and trim the greens, removing the roots and any bits of dirt. Coarsely chop them. You

Soup of Wild Greens *with* Gnocchi *and Prosciutto*

should have about 4 cups. In a large frying pan with a cover, heat the olive oil over medium heat, add the onion and chives, and sauté until the onion is just barely translucent. Add all the greens (they will barely fit), cover tightly, and cook over low heat until limp and considerably reduced in volume, 3 to 5 minutes.

In a blender or food processor, combine the greens and their juices with 1/2 cup of the chicken stock. Purée until smooth and transfer to a saucepan. Add the remaining 1 1/2 cups stock and heat, stirring often.

Meanwhile, bring a large pot of salted water to a boil. Add the fresh *gnocchi* and cook until they float to the surface, 2 or 3 minutes. If you are using dried *gnocchi*, cook them longer, about 10 minutes, or until just barely tender to the bite. Drain the *gnocchi*.

As soon as the *gnocchi* are done, ladle the soup into individual bowls. Top each serving with a few *gnocchi* and some prosciutto. Finish with some Romano cheese. Serve very hot.

Serves 4

Note: This soup becomes quite strong if allowed to sit. It should be eaten as soon as it is prepared.

SORREL AND POTATO SOUP

Spring is the best time to use sorrel. The long, sword-shaped leaves are bright green and as mildly sour as they will ever be. In the *potager* the leaves are not yet wilted by summer heat, and insects haven't nibbled the edges.

Quick and easy to make, this soup is a good choice to serve in the garden on a warm spring day, or inside by a fire if rain is pouring outside.

2 TABLESPOONS OLIVE OIL

1 TABLESPOON BUTTER

8 POTATOES, YELLOW FLESHED IF POSSIBLE,
    CUT INTO 1/2-INCH CUBES

2 LARGE LEEKS, INCLUDING TENDER GREEN
    PORTIONS, CHOPPED

2 QUARTS CHICKEN STOCK

15 LARGE OR 30 SMALL SORREL LEAVES, CUT
    INTO JULIENNE STRIPS

1/2 TEASPOON FRESHLY GROUND BLACK PEPPER

SALT TO TASTE

ABOUT 1/2 CUP *CRÈME FRAICHE* OR SOUR CREAM

2 TABLESPOONS FINELY CHOPPED FRESH CHIVE
    BLOSSOMS OR CHIVES FOR GARNISH

Sorrel and Potato Soup

In a stockpot large enough to hold the finished soup (a 4-quart pot will do), heat the olive oil and butter over medium heat. When the butter melts, add the potatoes and leeks and sauté gently until the leeks are translucent and the potatoes have begun to absorb the butter and oil, causing them to glisten. This will take 5 to 10 minutes. Add the chicken stock and cook until the potatoes are tender, 15 to 20 minutes longer.

About 5 minutes before the potatoes are done, add half of the sorrel and the pepper. Taste the soup for salt and adjust according to taste. When the potatoes are tender, remove the pot from the heat.

To serve, ladle some of the soup into each bowl and stir into each serving 2 or 3 tablespoons of the remaining sorrel. Top with a heaping tablespoonful of *crème fraîche* or sour cream and a sprinkling of the chive blossoms or chives. Serve at once.

Serves 4

Stew of Artichokes, Fava Beans, and Green Garlic

Most *potagers* in Provence have at least two artichoke plants and a row of eight or ten fava bean plants, which is enough to keep a family kitchen supplied with these important spring vegetables.

Provençal cooks prepare a traditional stew of artichokes and favas simmered with garlic and herbs at least once every spring. When I make it, I add green garlic as well, pulling my growing garlic plants just as the bases begin to swell and take on the appearance of green onions. Served with fresh bread and red wine, this rustic stew laden with the flavors of olive oil, garlic, and herbs is a country feast.

JUICE OF 1 LEMON, OR 1 TABLESPOON VINEGAR
16 VERY SMALL ARTICHOKES (ABOUT 2 OUNCES
      EACH), OR 6 MEDIUM-SIZED ARTICHOKES
2 TO 2 1/2 POUNDS YOUNG FAVA BEANS
      (ABOUT 2 CUPS SHELLED BEANS)
6 TO 8 GREEN GARLIC STALKS, OR 4 CLOVES
      GARLIC
1/2 CUP OLIVE OIL
2 TABLESPOONS CHOPPED FRESH WINTER SAVORY
2 TABLESPOONS CHOPPED FRESH THYME
1/2 TEASPOON SALT
1/2 TEASPOON FRESHLY GROUND BLACK PEPPER

Fill a large bowl with water and add the lemon juice or vinegar. If you are using small artichokes about the size of lemons, trim the stem end and cut off the top 1 inch of each artichoke. Peel away the outer layers of dark green leaves until you reach the pale yellow, tender

They are easily popped off by slitting the skin with the tip of a sharp knife or your thumbnail. Set the fava beans aside.

Cut each garlic stalk crosswise into 3 or 4 pieces. If using garlic cloves, mince them. Set aside.

Heat the olive oil in a heavy-bottomed saucepan over medium-high heat. Drain the artichoke pieces and dry them with paper towels. Add them to the pan and sauté for 3 or 4 minutes. Add the fava beans and the garlic and continue to cook for 10 minutes, stirring frequently. The artichokes will begin to change to deep olive green, but the favas will still be bright green.

Add the savory, thyme, salt, and pepper. Stir well, reduce the heat to very low, cover, and simmer until the artichokes are tender, 15 to 20 minutes.

Serves 4 to 6

ONION PANCAKES WITH DANDELION GREENS AND BACON

Golden savory pancakes, flecked with bits of green onion, are stacked in layers with bacon and wilted dandelion greens, and then drizzled with warm parsley butter. This simple, homey dish is perfect for a late breakfast, lunch, or supper.

Batter
1 CUP ALL-PURPOSE FLOUR
2 1/2 TEASPOONS BAKING POWDER
1/2 TEASPOON SALT
2 EGGS

inner leaves. Cut the artichoke in half, from stem to top, and remove any bits of furry choke. Cut the halves in half again lengthwise and drop the pieces into the water. To prepare medium-sized artichokes, trim the stem end and cut off the top 1 1/2 inches from each artichoke. Peel the outer leaves and halve as above. Remove any thistlelike leaves around the heart, as well as the fuzzy choke. Cut into sixths and drop into the water.

Shell the fava beans. Because some people are allergic to the skins of the fava beans and because they are somewhat tough, the skins should be removed, too.

1 1/4 CUPS MILK
3 TABLESPOONS BUTTER, MELTED AND COOLED
1/2 CUP FINELY CHOPPED GREEN ONIONS

VEGETABLE OIL FOR COOKING
1 BUNCH DANDELION GREENS OR SPINACH,
        STEMS REMOVED
16 SLICES BACON
6 TABLESPOONS BUTTER
1/4 CUP FINELY CHOPPED FRESH PARSLEY
JUICE OF 1/2 LEMON

To make the batter, sift the flour into a bowl. Return it to the sifter, add the baking powder and salt to the sifter, and resift the flour into the bowl.

Beat the eggs and milk together in a large bowl until well mixed. Stir in the butter, and then add the flour mixture. Beat the batter until it is smooth and free of lumps. Stir in the green onions. Preheat an oven to 200°F.

Heat a frying pan or griddle until it is medium-hot and grease it lightly with vegetable oil. For each pancake ladle about 1/4 cup of the batter into the heated pan or onto the griddle. Cook the pancakes until bubbles form on the tops and the bottoms are golden brown, 2 to 3 minutes. Turn and cook until the second side is golden, 2 to 3 minutes. Remove the pancakes to a heated dish and place in the oven. Repeat with the remaining batter. You should have 12 thin pancakes in all.

Arrange the greens on a steamer rack placed over gently boiling water. Cover and steam the greens until they are tender, 3 or 4 minutes. Remove the greens from the steamer and cut them lengthwise into julienne strips. Keep warm in the oven.

Meanwhile, cook the bacon in a frying pan over medium-high heat until crisp. Drain on paper towels and keep warm in the oven.

In a small pan melt the butter. Stir in the parsley and lemon juice and keep warm over very low heat.

For each serving, place a pancake on a dinner plate. Place a layer of the greens and 2 strips of the bacon on the pancake. Top with a second pancake and repeat the layering of the greens and bacon. Finally, place a third pancake on top. When all 4 of the pancake stacks are made, pour some of the warm parsley butter over each stack. Serve immediately.

Serves 4

Onion Pancakes with Dandelion Greens and Bacon

SAVORY BREAD PUDDING LAYERED WITH ASPARAGUS, FONTINA, AND MIXED SPRING HERBS

Save up your leftover bread for a week or so, especially the ends and slices from baguettes and any pieces of specialty breads such as *focaccia*. Let them get good and dry. Heavy, chewy breads make a dense pudding; lighter breads result in a softer, more traditional texture. Served with slices of smoky ham or grilled salmon fillets, this pudding is a good late breakfast or brunch dish.

12 TO 16 THICK SLICES DRY BREAD

2 1/2 TO 3 CUPS MILK

1 POUND ASPARAGUS

5 EGGS

1 TEASPOON SALT

1 TEASPOON FRESHLY GROUND BLACK PEPPER

1/4 CUP FRESHLY GRATED ROMANO CHEESE

4 OUNCES FONTINA CHEESE, SLIVERED

4 OUNCES SWISS CHEESE, SLIVERED

1/2 CUP CHOPPED MIXED FRESH HERBS, SUCH
     AS CHIVES, PARSLEY, AND TARRAGON,
     OR SAGE, THYME, AND MARJORAM

1 TABLESPOON BUTTER, CUT INTO SMALL BITS

Place the bread in a single layer in a shallow dish. Pour 2 1/2 cups milk over the top. Let soak until the bread has absorbed the milk and becomes soft, about 30 minutes. Press the bread slices to extract the milk. Measure the milk; you should have 1/2 cup milk left after squeezing. If not, make up the difference with the additional 1/2 cup milk as needed. Set the milk and bread aside.

While the bread is soaking, trim the asparagus, removing the woody ends. Cut the stalks on the diagonal into thin slivers each about 2 inches long and 3/8 inch thick. Arrange the slivered asparagus on a steamer rack and place over gently boiling water. Cover and steam until barely tender, 2 or 3 minutes. Immediately place the asparagus under cold running water until cold. Drain and set aside.

Preheat an oven to 350°F. Butter a 3-quart mold—a soufflé dish works well.

In a bowl beat together the eggs, salt, pepper, and the 1/2 cup milk until well blended. Layer one-third of the bread in the prepared dish. Set 6 to 8 asparagus slivers aside and top the bread layer with half of the remaining asparagus and half of the mixed herbs. Strew one-third of each of the cheeses over the asparagus. Repeat the layers, using half of the remaining bread, all of the remaining asparagus and herbs, and half of the remaining cheese. Arrange the remaining bread on top, strew the remaining cheese over it, and garnish with the reserved asparagus slivers. Pour the milk-egg mixture over the layers and then dot with the butter.

Bake in the preheated oven until the top is crusty brown and a knife inserted in the middle of the pudding comes out clean, about 45 minutes.

Serves 6 to 8

FETTUCCINE WITH PEA PODS AND MUSHROOMS

This is an ideal dish for garden-grown peas. Early in the season use the first young pods and some of the curly tendrils, which are surprisingly tender and sweet. Later on in the season use shelled mature peas. Young Chinese pea pods, or snow peas, available year-round, and the young peas that appear in the markets in the spring are good substitutes for home-grown peas.

The peas and mushrooms are cooked separately, then folded into the pasta along with the cream and cheese. Serve the fettuccine with hot, crusty bread.

1 CUP SMALL PEA PODS OR SHELLED PEAS (SEE NOTE)
5 TABLESPOONS BUTTER
1/2 CUP SLICED FRESH MUSHROOMS
2 1/2 TEASPOONS SALT
3 QUARTS WATER
12 OUNCES DRIED FETTUCCINE
2 TABLESPOONS HEAVY CREAM OR *CRÈME FRAICHE*
1/2 TEASPOON FRESHLY GROUND BLACK PEPPER
1/4 CUP FRESHLY GRATED PARMESAN CHEESE
2 TABLESPOONS CHOPPED FRESH CHIVES OR CHERVIL
1/4 CUP PEA TENDRILS (OPTIONAL)

If you are using pea pods, remove the tiny caps and any strings along the edges. Arrange the pea pods on a steamer rack over gently boiling water. Cover and steam for 1 minute. If you are using shelled peas, steam them in the same manner until they are tender, 10 to 15 minutes. Set the pea pods or peas aside. In a sauté pan melt 1 tablespoon of the butter over medium heat.

Fettuccine with Pea Pods and Mushrooms

Add the mushrooms and 1/2 teaspoon of the salt and sauté until just barely cooked, 2 to 3 minutes. Set aside.

Bring the water to a boil in a large pot and add 1 teaspoon of the salt. Add the fettuccine and cook until just barely done, 6 to 8 minutes. Drain thoroughly and transfer to a warmed serving bowl. Add the cream or *crème fraîche*, the remaining 4 tablespoons butter, the remaining 1 teaspoon salt, the pepper, cheese, and 1 tablespoon of the chives or chervil. Turn the fettuccine until it is well coated and all the butter has melted. Fold in the mushrooms and the pea pods or peas and the pea tendrils, if you are using them.

Garnish the dish with the remaining 1 tablespoon chives or chervil and serve hot.

Serves 4

Note: The pods, flowers, and tendrils of the sweet pea flower, *Lathyrus odoratus* are not edible under any circumstances and should not be confused with edible garden peas, *Pisum sativum*.

CHICKEN GALANTINE FILLED WITH SPRING GREENS AND MORELS

Despite their reputation, galantines are not necessarily difficult to make. With a little practice, you will soon feel so confident about filling a boned fowl with vegetables and meats, wrapping and tying it, and then poaching it that you will want to experiment with other seasonal combinations. I like to serve this galantine warm, after it has stood in the poaching liquid off the heat. Accompanied with pasta sauced with the poaching liquid and tossed with grated Parmesan cheese, it makes a very satisfying main dish, even though it doesn't correspond to the classic French presentation, which is a cold dish served as a first course. When served warm, it is closer to a *ballontine*, although in the strictest culinary sense a *ballontine* is meat that has been boned and rolled but not stuffed.

This galantine has the taste of spring. In the fall a galantine would be layered with wild cèpes instead of springtime morels, and the greens would be the slightly bitter chicories and kales.

Most butchers will readily bone a chicken when asked. Be sure to request that the meat and skin be left intact, in a single piece. Ask for the bones, gizzard, heart, and liver, all of which are used to make the stock in which the chard, spinach, and galantine are cooked.

Homemade galantines are very impressive dishes and never fail to win praise for the cook.

1 CHICKEN (3 1/2 TO 4 POUNDS), BONED,
WITH GIBLETS AND BONES
1 TEASPOON SALT
1 TEASPOON FRESHLY GROUND BLACK PEPPER
1 TEASPOON FRESHLY GRATED NUTMEG

Poaching Stock
2 TABLESPOONS BUTTER
1 ONION, CHOPPED
1 TEASPOON WHOLE BLACK PEPPERCORNS
2 CARROTS, HALVED
2 LEEKS, HALVED
3 STALKS CELERY
CHICKEN BONES AND GIBLETS FROM THE
BONED CHICKEN

Chicken Galantine Filled with Spring Greens and Morels

6 CUPS WATER
1/2 TEASPOON SALT

Filling

3 TABLESPOONS BUTTER
6 SHALLOTS, CHOPPED
6 FRESH MOREL MUSHROOMS, FINELY CHOPPED
1/4 CUP DRY WHITE WINE
12 TO 14 CHARD LEAVES, TRIMMED
1 POUND SPINACH, STEMS REMOVED
1 SMALL HEAD YOUNG ESCAROLE, TRIMMED
    AND SEPARATED INTO LEAVES
1/2 CUP FINE DRIED BREAD CRUMBS
1 TEASPOON MINCED FRESH THYME
1/2 TEASPOON SALT
1/2 TEASPOON FRESHLY GROUND BLACK PEPPER
1/4 TEASPOON FRESHLY GRATED NUTMEG
1/4 CUP CHOPPED FRESH PARSLEY
3 TABLESPOONS HEAVY CREAM

2 TABLESPOONS BUTTER

Lay the boned chicken on a flat surface, skin side down. Make a mixture of the salt, pepper, and nutmeg and rub the mixture over the meat surface of the chicken. Cover and refrigerate until ready to use.

To make the stock, in a stockpot melt the butter over medium heat. When it is foamy, add the onion and cook until translucent, 4 or 5 minutes. Add the peppercorns, carrots, leeks, and celery. (If you are growing celery in the garden, be sure to use it, as it gives a real punch to the stock that store-bought celery can't.) Cook the vegetables 1 or 2 minutes, stirring all the time. Add the bones and giblets, water, and salt and bring to a boil over high heat. Boil for 1 or 2 minutes, then reduce the heat and simmer the stock for 1 hour. Strain the stock and return it to the pot.

Begin to make the filling while the stock is cooking. Melt the butter in a sauté pan or frying pan over medium heat. Add the shallots and sauté until they are translucent, about 5 minutes. Add the mushrooms and cook slowly until tender, about 10 minutes. Remove the mushrooms and shallots from the pan with a slotted spoon and set aside. Add the white wine to the juices in the sauté pan and reduce the liquid over high heat by half. Remove the pan from the heat and return the mushrooms to the pan. Let them steep in the juices while you continue to prepare the other elements of the filling.

When the stock is ready, add the chard, spinach, and escarole to the simmering stock and cook for 2 or 3 minutes. Remove the leaves with a slotted spoon. Reserve several large chard leaves to use to line the inside of the chicken. Cut the remaining chard leaves and the spinach and escarole leaves into julienne strips. Set aside.

In a mixing bowl, combine the julienned greens, the mushrooms and their juices, the bread crumbs, thyme, salt, pepper, nutmeg, parsley, and cream.

Spread the chicken on a work surface, skin side down. Lay the reserved whole chard leaves atop the chicken, covering the surface completely. Shape the filling into a log and place it down the center of the chard-lined chicken. Starting on one side, roll up the chicken around the filling. With kitchen twine tie off the ends, then tie 2 or 3 pieces of twine around the circumference of the chicken to give it an even, cylindrical shape. Finally, make 1 or 2 lengthwise ties on the chicken.

In a frying pan large enough to hold the tied chicken, melt 2 tablespoons butter over medium heat.

Add the rolled chicken, increase the heat to medium high, and brown it evenly on all sides. This will take about 10 minutes.

While the chicken is browning, bring the poaching stock to a boil. As soon as the chicken is browned, gently slip it into the stock, cover, and reduce the heat to low. Poach the chicken for 30 minutes. Turn off the heat and let the galantine stand in the poaching liquid for 20 minutes.

Remove the galantine from the stock, clip and discard the twine, and cut it crosswise into 1/2-inch-thick slices. Alternatively, place the galantine on a plate, cover, and chill for several hours or overnight before serving.

Serves 6 to 8

GRILLED PORK CHOPS WITH MINT SOUFFLÉ

This combination is a showcase for fresh herbs. Rosemary accompanies the pork chops on the grill, and abundant amounts of mint, parsley, and chives are used in the soufflé. As the soufflé emerges from the oven, it fills the kitchen with the smell of garden-fresh herbs.

6 TO 8 LOIN OR CENTER-CUT PORK CHOPS,
ABOUT 1/2 INCH THICK
1 TEASPOON SALT
2 TABLESPOONS FRESHLY GROUND BLACK PEPPER
1 TABLESPOON OLIVE OIL
10 SPRIGS FRESH ROSEMARY (EACH 4 INCHES LONG)

Soufflé

4 EGGS, SEPARATED, PLUS 1 EGG WHITE

3 TABLESPOONS BUTTER

2 TABLESPOONS CHOPPED SHALLOTS

3 TABLESPOONS ALL-PURPOSE FLOUR

1/2 TEASPOON SALT

1 TEASPOON FRESHLY GROUND BLACK PEPPER

1 CUP MILK

1/4 CUP CHOPPED FRESH MINT

1 TABLESPOON CHOPPED FRESH PARSLEY

2 TABLESPOONS CHOPPED FRESH CHIVES

FRESH MINT SPRIGS FOR GARNISH

Rub the pork chops with the salt and pepper and set them aside. Rub the olive oil over the bottom of a large glass baking dish. Line the bottom of the dish with 5 of the rosemary sprigs. Place the chops on the sprigs, then top them with the remaining 5 rosemary sprigs. Cover the dish and let stand at room temperature for 2 or 3 hours.

To make the soufflé, preheat an oven to 400°F. At the same time, light a medium-hot fire in a charcoal grill or preheat a broiler.

Place the 5 egg whites in a bowl and beat until they form stiff peaks, 3 or 4 minutes. In a second bowl, place the egg yolks and beat them until they are well blended.

Grease a 3-cup soufflé mold with 1/2 table-spoon of the butter; set aside. Over medium heat, melt the remaining 2 1/2 tablespoons of butter in a heavy-bottomed saucepan large enough to hold the entire soufflé mixture eventually. Add the shallots and sauté until translucent, 2 or 3 minutes. Remove the pan from the heat and whisk in the flour, salt, and pepper until a paste forms. Return the pan to medium heat and gradually whisk in the milk in a steady stream. Reduce the heat to low and stir until there are no lumps. Simmer the sauce, stirring occasionally, until it becomes thick enough to coat the back of a spoon, about 10 minutes. Remove the pan from the heat once again and whisk in the egg yolks until the mixture is smooth and creamy. Then whisk in the mint, parsley, and chives and let cool for a few minutes. Stir one-fourth of the beaten egg whites into the egg yolk mixture. Carefully fold the remaining egg whites into the egg yolk mixture. Lastly, gently spoon the soufflé mixture into the prepared mold, filling it three-fourths full. Bake the soufflé at 400°F for 5 minutes, then reduce the heat to 375°F and bake until the soufflé is puffy and golden brown and a knife or a wooden skewer inserted in the center comes out clean, an additional 25 minutes.

About 15 minutes before the soufflé is ready, remove the pork chops and the rosemary from the marinade dish. Arrange the rosemary sprigs on the grill rack and place the pork chops on top. Alternatively, arrange the sprigs and chops on a broiler pan. Grill or broil until done, 4 to 5 minutes on each side.

Arrange the chops on a platter. Remove the soufflé from the oven and garnish the soufflé and the chops with the mint sprigs. Serve immediately, as the soufflé will collapse quickly once it is out of the oven.

Serves 4 to 6

MUSTARD-GLAZED SPRING CARROTS WITH SAGE LAMB CHOPS

As soon as the first carrots of spring are as big as my finger, I begin harvesting them. Small, delicate carrots are very tender and taste quite different from large carrots or those that have been topped and kept in storage. In the market you can readily spot freshly dug carrots because they still have their leafy green tops.

Before being glazed with a honey-mustard sauce, the carrots are steamed with half an inch or so of their green tops left on. The lamb chops are cooked atop a very thin bed of salt and fresh sage leaves in a very hot frying pan.

1/4 CUP HONEY MUSTARD
1 TABLESPOON BUTTER
JUICE OF 1 LEMON
1/2 TEASPOON SALT
12 TO 16 SMALL CARROTS, TOPS INTACT, 6 TO
    8 INCHES LONG
20 TO 30 FRESH SAGE LEAVES
4 LAMB SHOULDER CHOPS, ABOUT 1/2 INCH THICK
1/2 TEASPOON FRESHLY GROUND BLACK PEPPER
1/2 CUP WATER

In a saucepan large enough to hold the carrots, combine the mustard, butter, lemon juice, and a pinch of the salt. Cook over low heat until the butter melts and the mixture is thick enough to coat the back of a spoon, 10 to 15 minutes.

Trim the green tops from the carrots to within 1/2 inch of the crown. Arrange the carrots on a steamer rack over gently boiling water. Cover and steam until tender, 5 or 6 minutes.

Remove the carrots from the steamer and put them in the saucepan with the mustard sauce. Turn the carrots to coat each one completely with the sauce. Simmer the carrots over the lowest heat while you cook the chops.

In a frying pan large enough to hold all the chops at one time, sprinkle the remaining salt and all of the sage leaves. Heat the frying pan over high heat until the edges of the sage leaves begin to curl, about 2 minutes. Add the chops and sear them over high heat for 2 or 3 minutes on each side. Sprinkle with the pepper, then add the water and reduce the heat to low. Cover the pan and simmer for 5 minutes.

Put a lamb chop on each plate; be sure to include a few sage leaves and a spoonful of pan juices. Arrange 3 or 4 carrots in a fan on each plate and serve.

Serves 4

SAGE-ROASTED NEW POTATOES

In this easy-to-prepare recipe, new potatoes are first rubbed with olive oil, salt, and pepper, and then roasted with whole sage clusters. Their skins become crispy, while their centers turn soft and creamy. This contrast in texture, together with the fragrance and flavor of just-harvested sage, makes this an exceptional dish.

12 TO 15 NEW POTATOES, EACH ABOUT 1 1/2
INCHES IN DIAMETER
1/4 CUP OLIVE OIL

1 TEASPOON SALT
2 TEASPOONS FRESHLY GROUND BLACK PEPPER
10 TO 12 CLUSTERS FRESH SAGE

Preheat an oven to 350°F. Rub the potatoes with the olive oil, salt, pepper, and 2 of the sage clusters. Put the potatoes and all the sage clusters in an attractive oven-proof dish just large enough to hold them in a single layer. Bake until the potato skins are crispy and the centers are tender when pierced, about 1 hour.

Remove the potatoes from the oven and carry them directly to the table, sizzling hot.

Serves 4 or 5

Fresh Cherry Tart

Because I like cherry tarts that disguise that taste of the fresh fruits as little as possible, I usually bake a pastry crust and then cover it with snugly packed whole cherries. Sometimes I add a thin currant-jelly glaze to the base of the pastry before adding the fruit; other times I do nothing at all. A little heavy cream sweetened with confectioners' sugar serves as the topping. In France this tart is sometimes made with the pits still in the cherries, which makes eating it a rather daunting experience.

Pastry Shell
1 CUP ALL-PURPOSE FLOUR
2 TABLESPOONS SUGAR
1/4 TEASPOON SALT
6 TABLESPOONS UNSALTED BUTTER OR MARGARINE
1 EGG
1 TEASPOON VANILLA EXTRACT

1/2 CUP HEAVY CREAM
3 TABLESPOONS CONFECTIONERS' SUGAR
1/2 TEASPOON VANILLA EXTRACT
1 POUND VERY RIPE SWEET CHERRIES,
         STEMMED AND PITTED

To make the pastry shell, sift the flour, sugar, and salt together into a bowl. Using a pastry blender or 2 knives, cut the butter or margarine into the flour mixture until pea-sized balls form. Make a well in the center of the mixture and add the egg and vanilla. Mix quickly and lightly with a fork or your fingertips; do not overwork the dough or it will become sticky.

Gather the dough into a ball and wrap it in aluminum foil or waxed paper. Refrigerate for 15 or 20 minutes.

Preheat an oven to 350°F. Select a 9- or 10-inch tart pan that is 1 inch deep.

On a lightly floured surface, roll out the dough

Fresh Cherry Tart

into a round about 1/3 inch thick and 1 1/2 inches larger than the pan. Drape the pastry round over the rolling pin and transfer it to the tart pan. Unfold the dough and press it gently onto the bottom and sides of the pan.

Trim the dough even with the pan rim. Line the shell with aluminum foil. Add a layer of pastry weights or dried beans. Bake in the preheated oven for

Fraises au Vin Rouge *with Homemade Meringues*

10 minutes. Remove from the oven and lift out the weights and foil. Prick the bottom shell with the tines of a fork to allow steam to escape. Return the pastry shell to the oven and bake until lightly browned, about 10 minutes longer. Remove from the oven and let cool completely before filling.

Pour the cream into a bowl and stir in the con-fectioners' sugar and vanilla. Beat the cream until thick but not at all stiff. Cover and refrigerate the cream until you are ready to use it.

Arrange the cherries snugly on the pastry crust. Drizzle the sweetened cream over the cherries and serve at once.

Serves 6 to 8

FRAISES AU VIN ROUGE WITH HOMEMADE MERINGUES

Homemade meringue shells are a forgotten dessert that is worth reviving. In France sophisticated *vacherins*—meringues layered with ice cream or whipped cream—are purchased at the *glacière*, but I also remember the satisfying taste of the pale white meringues my mother made to hold my birthday ice cream.

Perfect meringues must be dry and crunchy. The surest way to achieve that end is to bake them at night and then leave them to dry in the oven until morning.

Top the meringues with the wine-marinated berries just as you serve them. The juice will soak in enough to flavor each crunchy bite— the taste sensation you want.

2 PINTS SMALL OR MEDIUM-SIZED STRAWBERRIES
1/4 TO 1/2 CUP SUGAR
1 TABLESPOON FRESH LEMON JUICE
1/4 TEASPOON VERY FINELY MINCED FRESH THYME
2 CUPS DRY RED WINE, SUCH AS A BURGUNDY
    OR ZINFANDEL

Meringue Shells
6 EGG WHITES
1/2 TEASPOON SALT
1 1/2 TEASPOONS CREAM OF TARTAR
1 1/2 CUPS SUGAR

Remove the green caps from the strawberries, but leave the berries whole. This shows that only perfect berries were used; slicing disguises that important part of the presentation. Place the berries in a bowl. Sprinkle the sugar over the berries. Use more or less sugar depending upon the sweetness of the fruit and your personal taste.

In a small bowl stir the lemon juice and thyme into the wine, and then pour the mixture over the strawberries. Refrigerate the berries for at least 3 or 4 hours before serving, or for up to 1 day. The longer the berries soak, the more wine flavored they will become.

To make the meringues, place the egg whites in a large stainless-steel bowl and let them come to room temperature. Preheat the oven to 250°F.

Add the salt and cream of tartar to the egg whites and beat until the mixture forms soft peaks. Add the sugar in small portions, about 2 tablespoons at a time, continuing to beat after each addition. As the sugar dissolves, the peaks will become increasingly stiff and glossy. Be careful not to overbeat and deflate the egg whites.

Line a baking sheet with a piece of ungreased brown paper—a section of a paper grocery bag, for example. To make each meringue, with a spoon scoop up approximately 3/4 cup of the egg white mixture and mound it on the lined baking sheet, forming a disk about 3 inches in diameter. With the back of a spoon, shape a well in the center. You should have 8 to 10 shells in all.

Bake the meringues in the preheated oven for 1 hour. At that point the shells will be dry and a very faint brown. Turn off the heat and let the meringues stand in the oven until they are completely cool, at least 2 hours or as long as overnight, if possible. Slip the meringues into a paper bag, fold over the top, and store them in a dry place until ready to use.

Just before serving, place a meringue shell on each serving plate and spoon some of the berries into the shell. Serve immediately.

Serves 8 to 10

SUMMER

Brochettes of Herbed Vegetables (page 65) and Grilled Sausages

SUMMER

The Season of Full Growth

he long, warm days of summer encourage the final cycle of plant growth, producing the thick-fleshed fruiting bodies that characterize the season's favorite vegetables. As a vegetable ripens, the seeds inside grow and begin to mature. In some instances the vegetable is considered at its culinary prime when the seeds are still quite immature, as in the case of summer squashes, cucumbers, and most eggplants. For tomatoes, melons, and sweet peppers, however, the culinary prime coincides with the maturation of the seeds at the end of the life cycle.

Summer's fruits come in a flood, beginning in June and lasting until the beginning of fall. Their periods of maturation overlap and by early August stone fruits, vine fruits, and pome fruits are all being harvested. Many of summer's tree-ripened stone fruits are highly perishable and have no season other than summer. Beginning at the end of June, the seasonal kitchen is inundated with nectarines, peaches, and plums. Come September the flush of stone fruits is over. Berry and melon vines start bearing shortly after the first nectarines and their fruits last into early fall. In late summer, apples and pears, the pome fruits, ripen along with grapes and the second crop of figs.

Seasonal cooking, whether *cuisine de marché* or *cuisine de potager*, is at its most colorful in summer. In the open markets it is possible to find a dozen or more different tomatoes. Heavy, lumpy, old-fashioned beefsteak types, red or yellow, are good for stuffing or slicing into salads. Tiny red or golden currant tomatoes, yellow and red cherry tomatoes, and green grape tomatoes can all be used whole. Red and yellow pear and plum tomatoes are bite-sized, too, and a cluster of them makes a little salad all on its own. Solid, thick-meated paste tomatoes, like the Romas and the San Marzanos cook down into dense sauces or make wonderful chopped tomato salads.

Sweet peppers are even more colorful than tomatoes. They come not only in shades of red, yellow, and green, but also in purple, orange, salmon, and deep chocolate. Green, purple, and chocolate peppers are in the immature stage of growth and will change colors and sweeten as they mature. Red, deep gold, and orange peppers are mature peppers whose flesh is heavier and more succulent than that of crisp immature peppers.

Each of the summer vegetables, from eggplants and beans to squashes, has a bright, distinct color, but I think glossy violet and lavender-and-white-striped eggplants are the most striking. With their spiky green caps and smooth globe shapes, they are so beautiful that I use them for table arrangements just as I would cut flowers.

For sheer brilliance and variety, though, even eggplants have difficulty competing with summer fruits. They come in every color of the rainbow and the fruit vendors capitalize on the colors to build kaleidoscopic displays. Shoppers, unable to resist, come closer, and then succumb to the fragrance of the ripe fruit. Plums alone come in shades of red, yellow, green, purple, and orange. Grapes display the same range of colors as plums, and the nectarines and peaches glow in shades of gold, yellow, and cream blushed with rose. Halved melons and watermelons lure buyers with sweet aromas and a spectrum of colors—oranges, yellows, golds, ivories, greens, and pinks. The summer market is alive with color and no one can scoop up enough fruit to make up for winter's dearth.

In the garden the intensity of summer colors is somewhat subdued by the green stalks, vines, and foliage that support the ripening vegetables and fruits. But bright masses of zinnias and bachelor buttons add a vibrant color dimension.

The summer garden has an allure all its own. Upon first glance, everything looks green. But plunge your hand in and start lifting leaves and pulling aside twining branches and vines and caches of fruiting color are revealed. For example, each year I cultivate a San Marzano tomato that tends to produce its fruits in handfuls of five or seven. The clusters are buried under overhangs of thick foliage. To the naked eye, there are no tomatoes, but to the experienced picker each overhang represents a potential treasure trove. The lifted vine reveals a cluster of tomatoes in one of three stages of growth: glossy, immature, lime-green tomatoes; light orange fruits in the process of turning red; or fully ripe, deep red tomatoes.

Summer cooking reflects the season. This is the time of the year when people play as much as possible, benefitting from the opportunity to be outside. Cooking tends to be simple, quick, or not at all. Many of summer's fresh foods are at their most delectable in their natural state. Platters of sliced vine-ripened tomatoes, cucumbers, and sweet peppers seasoned with fresh herbs and vinaigrettes, or trays of mixed melons and bowls of grapes and nectarines are summer salad basics. The same fruits and vegetables can be mixed into salads of cold grains or tossed with fresh farm cheeses.

Fresh beans, corn, and beets need to be steamed only briefly before eating them plain or combining them with other foods. Grilling is a summer pastime and vegetables grilled one night can be used the next day for a pizza topping or sandwich filling.

Soups, stews, and sauces are as light as summertime's salads and sandwiches. Ratatouille is the classic French stew made with the stars of the summer garden—tomatoes, eggplant, zucchini, and sweet peppers—and then served hot or cold the same day or the next night. Summer basil is the base for sauces of all kinds, while rosemary is the preeminent herb for grilling. Quickly made *aïoli*, laced with plenty of fresh garlic, is the seasonal spread that goes with everything from beets to tomato sandwiches.

Summer desserts are fruits, fruits, and more fruits, most often eaten alone, but sometimes accompanied with a cheese platter or cookies. When a prepared dessert seems called for, a *clafouti* of figs or peaches or a compote of wine-poached fruits scented with vanilla or lemon is a favorite choice.

Summer's overwhelming show of fruits and vegetables makes it possible to have the very best food cooked in the simplest ways. The ultimate summer cooking method is without doubt the barbecue grill. It is the culinary companion to summer's long, lazy days that beckon us outside and keep us there late into the warm evenings. The coming of fall with its crisp, chilly nights will soon send us back indoors.

RED AND YELLOW TOMATO PLATTER
WITH BALSAMIC VINEGAR

It is difficult to eat too many tomatoes during the summer. One of the best ways to present them is sliced, sprinkled with tarragon, and drizzled with olive oil and balsamic vinegar. Served with crusty chunks of bread to soak up the aromatic dressing, a big tomato platter is practically a meal in itself.

4 LARGE, VERY RIPE RED TOMATOES,
        THINLY SLICED
4 LARGE, VERY RIPE YELLOW TOMATOES,
        THINLY SLICED

1/4 CUP BALSAMIC VINEGAR
1/4 CUP OLIVE OIL
1/4 TEASPOON SALT
1/2 TEASPOON FRESHLY GROUND BLACK PEPPER
3 TABLESPOONS MINCED FRESH TARRAGON

Arrange the tomato slices in an overlapping single layer on a platter. First pour the vinegar evenly over them, and then the olive oil. Sprinkle with the salt, pepper, and, finally, the tarragon.

Let the dish stand at room temperature for 10 or 15 minutes to allow time for the flavors to mix.

Serves 6

ROAST CORN, RED PEPPER, AND OREGANO SALAD

The special flavor in this salad comes from using corn and sweet peppers roasted outdoors on a charcoal grill. The smoky taste of the vegetables combined with the sharp, slightly resinous taste of fresh oregano stirs up cultural memories of open spaces, sagebrush, and campfires. This salad is best eaten warm, when the corn and peppers are right off the grill.

8 EARS CORN, WHITE OR YELLOW, HUSK AND
    SILKS INTACT
1/3 CUP OLIVE OIL
4 RED BELL PEPPERS OR OTHER SWEET PEPPERS
1 TEASPOON SALT
1 TEASPOON FRESHLY GROUND BLACK PEPPER
1/4 CUP FINELY CHOPPED FRESH OREGANO

Prepare a fire in a charcoal grill. Remove the silks from the ears of corn, but leave the husks attached. Gently pull the husks back and brush the corn kernels with half of the olive oil; sprinkle them with half of the salt and black pepper. Pull the husks back into place.

Place the husk-wrapped corn and the red peppers on a medium-hot grill. Turn the peppers until the entire surface of each is scorched; this will take about 5 minutes. Remove the peppers and put them in a sealed plastic bag for a few minutes to sweat. Cook the corn for another 5 minutes. Peel back the husks and put the ears directly on the grill for 2 or 3 minutes, turning them often, to brown them a bit.

To finish the dish, cut off the kernels from each cob by running a sharp knife from the pointed end to the stem end. Place the kernels in a large bowl.

With your fingertips peel away the skins and remove the seeds and ribs from the peppers. Rinse the peppers under cold water and then cut them into thin slivers. Add the peppers to the bowl holding the corn, along with the oregano and the remaining olive oil, salt, and pepper. Toss gently and spoon into a serving dish.

Serves 6

Note: If you wish to add some greens to this salad, spinach is a good choice. It is not overwhelmed by the oregano and the bright green leaves are pretty with the red and yellow of the peppers and corn.

Ingredients for Roast Corn, Red Pepper, and Oregano Salad

COUSCOUS SALAD WITH

CHILI-MINT *HARISSA*

Properly speaking, couscous is semolina flour that is mixed with salted water, then formed into tiny round pellets, and finally cooked by steaming. Couscous is also a generic term for any of the numerous vegetable-and-meat stews of North African origin that are served with the grain, which is generally steamed over the simmering broth of the stew. The traditional accompaniment to these stews is *harissa*, a spicy sauce made from crushed dried chili peppers, olive oil, salt, and sometimes garlic and cumin, which is then thinned with broth from the simmering stew.

Couscous also makes a wonderful base for salads. Here the cooked, cooled grains are tossed with liberal amounts of chopped tomato, cucumber, and green onions, minced fresh mint and parsley, and a bit of olive oil, lemon juice, salt, and pepper. The spicy *harissa*

makes good use of the abundant mint in the garden and the last of the dried chilies from the previous summer.

In France I like to eat couscous salad with a side of *merguez*, a fiery North African sausage. In California I eat it with hot Polish or Italian sausages.

1 1/2 CUPS CHICKEN STOCK

1 1/2 CUPS COUSCOUS (SEE NOTE)

2 TABLESPOONS BUTTER, CUT INTO SMALL PIECES

5 1/2 TABLESPOONS OLIVE OIL

4 TOMATOES, PEELED, SEEDED, AND CHOPPED

3 CUCUMBERS, PEELED, SEEDED, AND CHOPPED

3 GREEN ONIONS, CHOPPED

1/4 CUP MINCED FRESH MINT

1/4 CUP MINCED FRESH PARSLEY

1/4 CUP FRESH LEMON JUICE

1/4 TEASPOON SALT

1/2 TEASPOON FRESHLY GROUND BLACK PEPPER

Harissa

1/4 CUP FRESH MINT LEAVES

2 CLOVES GARLIC, CRUSHED

1 CUP CHICKEN STOCK

1 SMALL, DRIED RED CHILI PEPPER, OR 2 FRESH SERRANO CHILI PEPPERS

SALT TO TASTE

FRESH MINT SPRIGS FOR GARNISH

Bring the chicken stock to a boil in a medium-sized saucepan. Stir in the couscous, cover, and cook over very low heat for 5 minutes. Remove the pan from the heat and let the couscous stand, covered, until all the liquid has been absorbed, about 5 minutes. Add the butter to the couscous and fluff carefully with a fork to separate the

Rosemary Pizzas

grains. I use my fingertips as well. Add 1 1/2 tablespoons of the olive oil and fluff again. The idea is for each pellet to be separate and fluffy. Let cool to room temperature.

Add the tomatoes, cucumbers, green onions, mint, and parsley to the couscous and fluff the ingredients together. In a small bowl mix together the remaining 4 tablespoons olive oil, the lemon juice, salt, and pepper. Pour it over the couscous mixture. Fluff one more time. Set the salad aside.

To make the *harissa*, in a small saucepan bring the mint, garlic, and chicken stock to a boil. Reduce the heat and simmer for 10 minutes. Remove and discard the stems and seeds from the dried or fresh chilies and add the chilies to the stock. Increase the heat to high and reduce the stock mixture by half, which will take 5 to 10 minutes. Transfer the mixture to a blender or food processor and purée until smooth.

Serve the salad chilled or at room temperature. Garnish with mint sprigs. Serve the *harissa* on the side in a separate bowl.

Serves 4 to 6

Note: Do not use instant (precooked) couscous, as it is difficult to fluff up.

ROSEMARY PIZZAS

Topped with lots of fresh rosemary, thinly sliced fresh tomatoes, and thin shavings of dry *parmigiano-reggiano* or Monterey jack cheese, these thin-crusted pizzas are as simple as summer itself. Experiment with other herbs and other summer vegetables, such as roasted eggplant or red sweet peppers, to make your own versions.

Crust

2 ENVELOPES (SCANT 1 TABLESPOON EACH)
ACTIVE DRY YEAST
1 CUP WARM WATER (105°F)
1 TEASPOON SUGAR
1 TEASPOON SALT
2 TABLESPOONS OLIVE OIL
ABOUT 3 1/2 CUPS ALL-PURPOSE FLOUR
2 TABLESPOONS CORNMEAL FOR PAN

Topping

4 TO 5 TABLESPOONS OLIVE OIL
2 LARGE RED OR YELLOW TOMATOES, SLICED
1/4 INCH THICK
12 SALT-CURED BLACK OLIVES
1/2 CUP SHAVED PARMIGIANO-REGGIANO OR
OTHER DRY AGED CHEESE
4 TABLESPOONS CHOPPED FRESH ROSEMARY

A food processor is ideal for making the pizza crust, although it can be made by hand. In a small bowl, dissolve the yeast in the warm water. Add the sugar and let stand until foamy, about 5 minutes.

In a food processor bowl fitted with a metal blade, combine the yeast mixture, salt, 1 tablespoon of the olive oil, and 3 cups of the flour. Process until the ingredients come together into a ball. If the dough is too wet, add more flour, a little at a time, until a smooth, firm texture is achieved. Continue to process for 3 to 4 minutes after the ball is formed, or until the dough is smooth and silky but firm. Turn the dough out onto a well-floured board and knead until the dough becomes elastic, 4 or 5 minutes.

If preparing the dough by hand in a bowl, follow the same steps, but use only 2 cups of flour instead of 3 cups to start and work the ingredients together with a fork or your fingertips. Gradually add more flour until the dough forms a stiff ball. Turn the dough ball out onto a well-floured board and knead it until it becomes smooth and elastic. This will take 6 or 7 minutes.

Oil a large bowl with the remaining 1 tablespoon olive oil. Place the dough ball in the bowl and turn the ball to coat the surface with oil. Cover the bowl with a clean cloth and let stand in a warm place until the dough has doubled in size, 1 to 1 1/2 hours. Punch down the dough in the bowl, re-cover it with the cloth, and let it rest for another 30 minutes.

Preheat an oven to 500°F. Divide the dough into 2 or 4 equal portions, depending upon the number of pizzas you are making. On a lightly floured board, roll out each portion into a round 1/8 inch thick. If you are making 2 pizzas, each round should be about 12 inches in diameter. If you are making 4 pizzas, each round should be about 6 inches in diameter. Sprinkle the pizza pans or large baking sheets with the cornmeal and transfer the dough rounds to the pans.

To top the pizzas, drizzle half of the olive oil over the surface of the dough rounds. Divide the tomato slices and olives evenly among the dough rounds. Strew the cheese over the tomato slices and then sprinkle with 2 tablespoons of the rosemary. Cook the pizzas on the upper rack of the oven until the bottom of the crust is crisp and the edges are lightly browned, 10 or 12 minutes.

Remove the pizzas from the oven. Drizzle with the remaining 2 to 2 1/2 tablespoons olive oil, then sprinkle with the remaining 2 tablespoons rosemary. Cut the larger pizzas into wedges and leave the smaller pizzas whole. Serve immediately.

Makes two 12-inch or four 6-inch pizzas; serves 4

CREAM OF RATATOUILLE SOUP WITH

SAVORY CROUTONS

Out of the high summer garden come the purple and lavender eggplants, colorful peppers, tomatoes, and zucchini that are the basis for ratatouille, the classic vegetable stew of a Provence summer. In this variation, the ratatouille is coarsely chopped or puréed and then mixed with chicken stock and a bit of cream to transform it from a stew into a soup. Big, golden herbed-flecked croutons go on top, where they immediately begin to soak up the summer flavors. Serve extra croutons in a separate bowl; they will disappear quickly.

3 TABLESPOONS OLIVE OIL

2 CLOVES GARLIC, CHOPPED

1 EGGPLANT, PEELED AND CUT INTO 1-INCH CUBES

1 ZUCCHINI, CUT INTO 1-INCH CUBES

1 LARGE ONION, QUARTERED

1 LARGE RED, GREEN, OR YELLOW BELL PEPPER
    OR OTHER SWEET PEPPER, SEEDED,
    DERIBBED, AND CUT INTO 1-INCH SQUARES

4 LARGE, VERY RIPE TOMATOES, PEELED AND
    QUARTERED

ABOUT 1 CUP CHICKEN STOCK

1/2 TEASPOON SALT

1 TEASPOON FRESHLY GROUND BLACK PEPPER

2 TABLESPOONS FINELY CHOPPED FRESH THYME

2 TABLESPOONS HEAVY CREAM

2 CUPS SAVORY CROUTONS (PAGE 29)

RED AND YELLOW BELL PEPPER OR OTHER SWEET
    PEPPER SLIVERS FOR GARNISH

Heat 2 tablespoons of the olive oil in a heavy-bottomed, medium-sized saucepan. Add the garlic and sauté until translucent. Add the eggplant, zucchini, onion, and bell pepper and cook over medium heat until the vegetables are slightly soft, 10 or 15 minutes. Add the tomatoes and the remaining 1 tablespoon olive oil. Cook, stirring frequently, until the vegetables are well mixed and the tomatoes begin to dissolve, 15 to 20 minutes. Reduce the heat to low, cover, and cook for an additional 15 minutes, stirring occasionally.

Remove the mixture from the heat and let cool for 5 or 10 minutes. Add the entire contents of the saucepan to a blender or food processor and purée until smooth. Return the mixture to the saucepan and add as much of the chicken stock as needed to create a mixture with the consistency of a thick pea soup. The amount of stock needed will depend upon the juiciness of your tomatoes. Add the salt, pepper, and thyme. Bring the mixture to just below a boil, stirring constantly. Remove from the heat and swirl in the cream. Taste and adjust the seasoning, if necessary.

Serve the soup hot garnished with croutons and thin slivers of pepper.

Serves 4 to 6

FISH SOUP WITH PERNOD *PISTOU*

This Provençal fish soup is as traditional as its more famous relative, bouillabaisse. It is, however, far less fancy and far less complex to make, as I learned one July afternoon.

Maurice Luchesi always has a few free days in July before the melons ripen, and he likes to spend them fishing. On this day he returned in the late afternoon from fishing off the rocks near Toulon on the Mediterranean. He had brought back what seemed to me a paltry collection of fish too small and too bony to eat. Françoise, however, was quite pleased with the catch and announced she would make soup. I watched her carefully, as I had eaten this soup in a nearby restaurant and had thought it delicious.

I was surprised to learn how easy it was to make. The principals are these: any number of small fish or pieces of large fish from the ocean are cooked whole in olive oil with herbs, potatoes, tomatoes, stock, and fennel stalks. The entire mixture then goes through a food mill twice, after which it is reheated and served with a big piece of garlic-rubbed toast and a spicy sauce. In this version, the sauce is a *pistou* enlivened with Pernod instead of the traditional *rouille* of red peppers, olive oil, and garlic thickened with bread.

Although I once had a *poissonière* in France refuse to sell me fish for soup because in her opinion they were not the correct ones, I find that almost any kind of ocean fish makes a good fish soup. In fact Françoise even makes fish soup with freshwater fish and adds a few anchovies to salt it up!

6 TABLESPOONS OLIVE OIL

1 POUND MIXED SMALL ROCKFISH OR COMBINATION
    OF SMALL FISH AND PIECES OF LARGER FISH

5 CLOVES GARLIC

2 ONIONS, QUARTERED

6 POTATOES, SLICED 1/2 INCH THICK

2 BAY LEAVES

6 SPRIGS FRESH THYME, OR 1 TABLESPOON
    DRIED THYME

8 LARGE, VERY RIPE TOMATOES, QUARTERED

4 CUPS HOMEMADE FISH STOCK OR CHICKEN
    STOCK OR BOTTLED CLAM JUICE

1 CUP WATER

4 PIECES FENNEL STALK, HALF OF A FENNEL
    BULB, OR 1 TABLESPOON FENNEL SEED

1/2 TEASPOON SALT

1/2 TEASPOON FRESHLY GROUND BLACK PEPPER

Pistou

1/4 CUP OLIVE OIL

3 CLOVES GARLIC

1/4 CUP UNSALTED ALMONDS

1 CUP FRESH BASIL LEAVES

1/2 TEASPOON SALT

1/4 TEASPOON FRESHLY GROUND BLACK PEPPER

1/4 CUP PERNOD

8 SLICES FRENCH BREAD, TOASTED

In a soup pot over medium heat, warm 4 tablespoons of the olive oil. Add the fish, 2 of the garlic cloves, and the onions. Cook, stirring, until the fish begin to change color and fall apart. Add the potatoes, bay leaves, and thyme and continue cooking over medium heat for 5 minutes, stirring and scraping frequently to prevent burning. Stir in the tomatoes. Add 2 cups of the stock and scrape up any bits stuck to the bottom of the pan. Add the remaining 2 cups stock, the water, fennel or fennel seed, salt, and pepper. Cover and cook over low heat until the potatoes are tender, about 30 minutes.

Position a food mill or a large, fine-mesh strainer over a bowl. Pour the contents of the soup pot into the mill or strainer and press it through to the bowl. The fish bones, herb sprigs, and tomato skins will be trapped, leaving a smooth, thick purée in the bowl.

Discard the contents of the mill or strainer and rinse thoroughly. Pass the puréed soup through the cleaned mill or strainer again, to eliminate any bones that might have slipped through the first time around. Transfer the puréed soup to a saucepan and set aside.

To make the *pistou,* combine the olive oil, garlic, and almonds in a blender or food processor. Process until a paste forms. Add the basil and continue to process until the basil leaves have been completely incorporated into the paste. Add the salt, pepper, and Pernod. Process until a rather thick sauce forms. Set aside.

Bring the puréed soup to a boil. Reduce the heat and simmer for 5 minutes, stirring frequently.

Ingredients for Fish Soup with Pernod Pistou

Meanwhile, preheat a broiler. Rub the toasted bread slices with the remaining 2 garlic cloves and then drizzle the toasts with the remaining 2 tablespoons olive oil. Put the bread slices under the broiler until lightly golden, 2 to 3 minutes.

To serve, ladle the hot soup into individual bowls. Top each bowl with a small spoonful of sauce. Put the remaining sauce in a bowl. Serve the garlic toasts and the sauce along with the soup.

Serves 4 to 6

PROVENÇAL STUFFED VEGETABLES

All summer long, eggplants, zucchini, sweet red peppers, and tomatoes filled with a flavorful stuffing of sausage, herbs, and spicy bread crumbs are served in country restaurants and at family meals.

One summer I was at a restaurant in Saint-Rémy, near Avignon. It was late summer and only about three quarters of the tables on the terrace were filled. The heavy shade of the quintessential plane trees lining the street kept us cool as we drank chilled Provençal rosé and savored the mixed stuffed vegetables. They were brought to us family style, since we had both ordered them. Eggplants, tomatoes, squashes, sweet peppers, and onions had been arranged in rows in a glazed terra-cotta baking dish and then garnished with fresh basil sprigs.

Two days later we were invited to a neighbor's home for dinner. After a first course of pâté and *jambon cru*, our hosts told us that we were having stuffed vegetables because they were so typically Provençal and soon the season for eggplants, tomatoes, and peppers would be over.

4 CUPS CUBED DRY BREAD (2-INCH CUBES)

3 CUPS MILK

3 RED BELL PEPPERS

1 LARGE GLOBE EGGPLANT, OR 4 SMALL
    ASIAN EGGPLANTS

4 SMALL ZUCCHINI (EACH ABOUT 4
    INCHES LONG)

4 TOMATOES

1 1/2 POUNDS BULK PORK SAUSAGE MEAT

4 CLOVES GARLIC, CHOPPED

1 ONION, CHOPPED

3 MEDIUM-SIZED EGGS, BEATEN

1/4 CUP CHOPPED FRESH PARSLEY

1/4 CUP CHOPPED FRESH THYME

2 TEASPOONS FRESHLY GROUND BLACK
PEPPER, OR TO TASTE

1 TEASPOON SALT, OR TO TASTE

Put the bread cubes and the milk in a bowl to soak while you prepare the vegetables.

Cut the red peppers in half lengthwise and discard the seeds and the ribs. Set aside. Cut the large eggplant or small eggplants in half lengthwise. Scoop out the pulp, forming shells 1/3 inch thick. Put the scooped-out meat in a mixing bowl. Cut the zucchini in half lengthwise and scoop out the pulp, forming shells 1/3 inch thick. Add the pulp to the bowl holding the eggplant pulp. Set the eggplant and zucchini shells aside with the red peppers.

Cut the tomatoes in half and scoop out a heaping tablespoonful of meat from the center of each half. Put 2 scoops of the tomato in a small bowl to use later; discard the rest or reserve for another use. Put the tomato shells with the other vegetable shells.

Preheat an oven to 350°F. Finely chop the eggplant and zucchini pulp and return it to the bowl. Squeeze the milk from the bread, then add the bread to the bowl along with the sausage meat, garlic, onion, eggs, parsley, thyme, black pepper, salt, and the reserved tomato pulp. Mix well, then fry a small bit of the mixture and taste for seasoning. If it tastes too bland, add more salt and pepper.

Fill each of the vegetable shells with some of the sausage mixture. The stuffing should mound slightly in the shells, as it will shrink as it cooks. Place the stuffed vegetables on a large, ungreased baking sheet and bake in the preheated oven for 35 to 45 minutes. The vegetable shells should be tender but not collapsing.

Serve the vegetables hot or at room temperature. They are also good picnic fare and travel well.

Serves 6

BROCHETTES OF
HERBED VEGETABLES AND
TAPENADE TOASTS

Cooked quickly over a grill, each of the summer vegetables that makes up these brochettes maintains its own distinct taste. The toasts, spread with thick, olive-and-anchovy-rich *tapenade*, cook to a deep brown and are an excellent flavor match with the vegetables.

The greater variety in kind and color of vegetables, the more spectacular the brochettes will be. Beets grill beautifully after precooking, and their ruby-red color sets off purple-edged eggplants and brilliant orange and yellow peppers.

Use very fine metal or wooden skewers. The crisp vegetables will thread more easily and with less chance of breaking than if thick, flat skewers are used.

Serve the brochettes with grilled sausages. *Merguez*, a spicy North African sausage, is my choice in France. Here I like chicken-apple sausages or any kind made with garlic or fennel.

4 BEETS
1 GLOBE EGGPLANT
6 SUMMER SQUASHES, IN AN ASSORTMENT
    SUCH AS ZUCCHINI, YELLOW
    CROOKNECK, AND PATTYPAN
4 BELL PEPPERS OR OTHER SWEET PEPPERS,
    IN A VARIETY OF COLORS
3 LARGE RED ONIONS
12 GREEN BEANS
1/4 CUP OLIVE OIL
1/4 CUP CHOPPED FRESH BASIL
1/2 CUP FRESH ROSEMARY LEAVES
1/2 TEASPOON SALT
1/2 TEASPOON FRESHLY GROUND BLACK PEPPER

Tapenade

1 CUP PITTED BLACK OLIVES
8 FLAT ANCHOVY FILLETS IN OIL, DRAINED
1/4 CUP DRAINED CAPERS
1 HEAPING TABLESPOON DIJON-STYLE MUSTARD
2 TABLESPOONS OLIVE OIL
12 SLICES FRENCH BREAD, ABOUT 1/2 INCH THICK

Trim the stems from the beets, leaving about 1/2 inch on each. Place the beets in a saucepan, add water to cover, and bring to a boil. Boil the beets until just tender when pierced with a fork, about 20 minutes depending upon the size of the beets. Drain, cool, and slip off the skins. Cut the beets into slices 3/8 inch thick. Place in a bowl and set aside.

Cut the eggplant crosswise into 3/8-inch-thick rounds. Halve the rounds. Cut the squashes lengthwise into halves or thirds, depending upon their size, and then cut the pieces crosswise in half. Cut the peppers from top to bottom into 3 or 4 large pieces. Remove the seeds and ribs. Slice the onions crosswise into rounds 3/8 inch thick. Trim the beans and cut each into 2-inch-long pieces.

Put all of the vegetables except the beets into a bowl and add the olive oil, basil, rosemary, salt, and pepper, reserving a little bit of each for marinating the beets. Toss to mix well. Add the reserved marinade ingredients to the beets and toss well. Marinate the vegetables for 1 hour.

If you are using wooden skewers, soak 12 skewers in water to cover for about 30 minutes. Light a fire in a charcoal grill.

While the vegetables are marinating, prepare the *tapenade*. In Provence, *tapenade* is traditionally prepared with salt-cured olives that have been packed in olive oil. The olives and all the other ingredients are crushed and blended into a paste by hand in a marble mortar with a pestle. If you lack salt-cured olives and a marble mortar, an acceptable version of *tapenade* can be made with well-drained canned black olives in a blender.

Put the olives and the anchovies in a blender or food processor and chop them. Add the capers and chop again. Finally add the mustard and olive oil and blend to a paste. Cut the slices of bread in half to make half-moons. Spread both sides of the bread slices with the paste and set aside.

To assemble the brochettes, skewer the vegetables and the breads to expose the maximum surface to the grill, alternating types and colors of vegetables with half-moons of the *tapenade*-covered bread. Fill 1 skewer with *tapenade*-covered bread slices only.

Cook the brochettes over a medium-hot fire for 3 to 4 minutes per side. Serve hot.

Serves 4 to 6

Basil-Chicken Ravioli with Red and Green Sauces

Unless you have strong and practiced arms capable of rolling a sheet of dough to an almost transparent thinness, I recommend using an inexpensive manual pasta machine. I love mine. I constantly marvel at how beautifully it turns a goose egg of dough into delicate, thin sheets of pasta. Eating one night at a fresh-pasta restaurant near the port in Nice, I was astonished to see a little pasta machine, just like mine, turning out the dough for the made-to-order ravioli—in my case, stuffed with huge, tender slices of *fonds des artichauts*.

Ravioli can be filled with almost anything, but in summertime the abundance of fresh basil makes it a natural choice. Double the taste of fragrant basil with a pestolike green sauce and add another sauce made with roasted red peppers and tomatoes and your pasta feast is accomplished.

Green Sauce
1 cup fresh basil leaves
1/4 cup olive oil
1/4 cup freshly grated Parmesan cheese
2 tablespoons blanched almonds
1/2 teaspoon salt

Red Sauce
1 large red bell pepper or other sweet pepper
2 medium-sized tomatoes
2 cloves garlic, unpeeled
1/4 cup olive oil
1/4 teaspoon salt
1/2 teaspoon freshly ground black pepper

Basil-Chicken Ravioli with Red and Green Sauces

Filling

2 CUPS FRESH BASIL LEAVES, MINCED

1 CUP MINCED COOKED CHICKEN

1/2 CUP FINE DRIED BREAD CRUMBS

1/4 TEASPOON SALT

1/8 TEASPOON FRESHLY GRATED NUTMEG

1 EGG

Ravioli Dough

2 CUPS ALL-PURPOSE FLOUR

1/2 TEASPOON SALT

3 EGGS

FRESHLY GRATED PARMESAN CHEESE FOR SERVING

To make the green sauce, combine the basil leaves and the olive oil in a blender or food processor. Purée until smooth. Add the cheese, almonds, and salt and process until all the ingredients are well blended into a sauce. If the sauce seems too thick, add a little more olive oil. Set aside.

To make the red sauce, preheat an oven to 450°F or prepare a fire in a charcoal grill. Roast the red peppers, tomatoes, and garlic cloves in the preheated oven or on a grill over a medium-hot charcoal fire until slightly charred on all sides, about 5 minutes. Remove the vegetables and garlic from the oven or grill. Put the peppers in a sealed plastic bag for a few minutes to sweat. With your fingertips peel away the skins and remove the seeds and ribs. Remove the skin and core from the tomatoes. Place the garlic cloves and olive oil in a blender or food processor and purée. Add the peppers, tomatoes, salt, and black pepper and purée until smooth. Set aside.

To make the filling, combine all the ingredients in a mixing bowl. Mix the ingredients with a fork until they are moistened just enough to hold together. Cover and refrigerate while you prepare the ravioli dough.

I think the easiest way to make ravioli dough is in a food processor. Put the flour in first, then the salt, and finally the eggs. Process until a sticky ball forms. Place the dough ball on a floured board and knead about 7 minutes until the dough is elastic.

To make the dough by hand, pile the flour on a pastry board or in a bowl and make a well in the center of the flour. Put the salt and the eggs in the well. With your fingertips or a fork, work the flour into the eggs gradually, starting in the center and moving toward the edges of the flour wall. Continue working the dough until a sticky ball forms. Knead as described above.

Wrap the dough loosely in plastic wrap or aluminum foil and let stand at room temperature for 30 minutes or so. Once the dough has rested, divide it in half.

Flour the largest work surface you have. On the floured surface, roll out half of the dough into a rectangle about 1/16 inch thick, 18 inches on one side, and 24 inches on the other. Visualize the sheet of dough as divided into 2-by-2-inch squares. Place a teaspoonful of filling in the middle of each square. Roll out the remaining dough in the same way. Place the second sheet of dough over the first. With the palm of your hand, gently pat the tops of the lumps of filling. With the edge of your hand, press the upper sheet to the lower one, making lines between the filling lumps, to seal the edges of the ravioli. With a pastry cutter or sharp knife, cut along each sealing line, dividing the filled dough into approximately 2-inch squares.

The ravioli are now ready to cook. If, however, you want to wait several hours before cooking them, arrange them in a single layer, not touching, on a flour-dusted cloth or piece of waxed paper. Dust the ravioli with flour and cover with another cloth or piece of waxed paper.

To cook the ravioli, bring a large pot of salted water to a boil. Drop the ravioli in batches into the boiling water; do not crowd too many into the pot at once. Cook for 3 to 4 minutes, or until the ravioli pop to the surface. Do not overcook. Remove the ravioli with a slotted spoon to a warmed platter.

When all of the ravioli are cooked, serve immediately with the sauces and extra Parmesan cheese.

Makes approximately 100 ravioli; serves 6 to 8

CHARRED EGGPLANT SANDWICHES
WITH *Aïoli*

When eggplant slices are flawlessly grilled, they have golden brown crusts and creamy interiors. The slices make ideal sandwich fillings and can be stored for a day or two in the refrigerator. Be sure to use very good, very fresh, chewy bread for the best sandwiches.

2 GLOBE EGGPLANTS
1/4 CUP OLIVE OIL
1/4 CUP MIXED FRESH HERB LEAVES, SUCH AS
     THYME, ROSEMARY, AND OREGANO
1/4 TEASPOON SALT
1/2 TEASPOON FRESHLY GROUND BLACK PEPPER

broiler. Arrange the eggplant slices on the grill rack or on a broiler pan and grill or broil the slices until a crust forms on the first side. Turn the slices and cook for 3 or 4 minutes longer.

Slice the rolls or baguettes open and spread the cut sides with the *aïoli*. Add 2 eggplant slices and 1 or 2 pieces butter lettuce. Replace the tops and serve.

Serves 6

Sautéed Corn off the Cob and Shell Beans

Maurice Luchesi is one of the few market growers in Provence to grow and sell sweet corn, which is not a traditional French food. He was introduced to it by an American couple and has been growing and eating it for almost a decade. Starting sometime in July, he packs his Renault 4L wagon full of ears of Sweet Illini and Platinum Lady and heads off to the daily markets, where he sells out immediately. When I cook this quick sauté in France, I use classic French *flageolet* beans with the corn, since Maurice isn't growing lima beans yet.

This is a good side dish to serve with barbecued steaks, chops, or chickens.

Simple Aïoli

2 CLOVES GARLIC

1 TABLESPOON OLIVE OIL

1/4 TEASPOON CHOPPED FRESH THYME

3/4 CUP HOMEMADE OR COMMERCIAL MAYONNAISE

6 CHEWY ROLLS; OR 2 BAGUETTES, EACH CUT
CROSSWISE INTO THIRDS

6 TO 12 BUTTER LETTUCE LEAVES

Trim the eggplants and cut them crosswise into slices 3/8 inch thick. You should have 12 slices in all. Combine the olive oil, herbs, salt, and pepper in a shallow dish. Add the eggplant slices and turn to coat well. Marinate for half an hour or more.

Prepare my simplified version of *aïoli* while the eggplant is marinating. In a blender or food processor, combine the garlic, olive oil, and thyme. Purée until smooth. Add the mayonnaise and process until just blended. The longer the mayonnaise stands, the stronger the garlic flavor will become.

Prepare a fire in a charcoal grill or preheat a

1 CUP FRESH SHELL BEANS, SUCH AS
FLAGEOLET, LIMA, OR CRANBERRY

3 EARS CORN, WHITE OR YELLOW

2 TABLESPOONS BUTTER

1 TEASPOON OLIVE OIL

1 CLOVE GARLIC, CRUSHED AND THEN MINCED

Overleaf: *Charred Eggplant Sandwiches with Aïoli*

1/4 TEASPOON SALT

1/4 TEASPOON FRESHLY GROUND BLACK PEPPER

1 TABLESPOON FINELY CHOPPED FRESH BASIL

Arrange the beans on a steamer rack over gently boiling water. Cover and steam the beans until they are tender. The length of time needed will vary depending upon the type and the age of the beans. Lima beans and cranberry beans will take approximately 20 minutes; *flageolet* beans will take slightly less. When the beans are cooked, remove them from the steamer and set aside.

Meanwhile, fill a large pot with water and bring it to a boil. Drop in the corn and cook for no more than 3 or 4 minutes. Drain the corn and cool slightly until it can be handled. Using a sharp knife, cut off the kernels from each cob by running a sharp knife from the pointed end to the stem end. Set aside.

Heat the butter and olive oil in a saucepan over medium-high heat. Add the garlic and cook, stirring, for 2 or 3 minutes. Add the corn, beans, salt, and pepper and cook, stirring frequently, for 5 minutes. Stir in the basil and serve hot.

Serves 4 to 6

Corn off the Cob and Shell Beans

FRESH FIG *CLAFOUTI*

When I was first living in the French countryside, an old *mémé* who lived down the road brought me a chipped small, white plate covered with fig leaves and five bright green, very plump, perfect figs. When I asked her where the figs had come from, she showed me an old twisted tree at the edge of an abandoned orchard half-hidden by a tangle of weeds. She explained that although the tree never had many figs, they were always very good.

Dozens of different varieties of figs exist and all of them have their own characteristics. When I make this custardlike *clafouti*, I mix as many fig varieties together as I can: large, green, golden-meated ones, small green ones with strawberry interiors, and large and small purple ones with pale rose centers.

Halved and soaked in a syrup of brown sugar and Marsala, then packed closely together on top of the custard, almost touching, some face up, some face down, the figs make a rich pattern of color that bakes into the custard.

18 TO 20 SMALL, 16 TO 18 MEDIUM-SIZED,

OR 10 LARGE FIGS

1/4 CUP BROWN SUGAR

1/4 CUP MARSALA WINE

2 TABLESPOONS WATER

Batter

1 CUP MILK

1/4 CUP PLUS 2 TABLESPOONS HEAVY CREAM

1/4 CUP FIRMLY PACKED BROWN SUGAR

3 EGGS

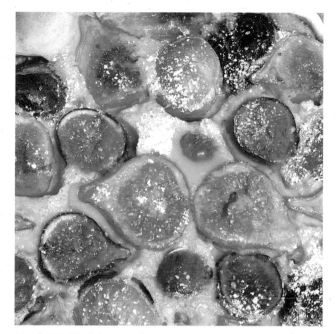

Fresh Fig Clafouti

1 TABLESPOON VANILLA EXTRACT

1/8 TEASPOON SALT

2/3 CUP ALL-PURPOSE FLOUR, SIFTED

CONFECTIONERS' SUGAR (OPTIONAL)

Halve small or medium-sized figs and quarter large ones; set aside. In a medium-sized saucepan, bring the brown sugar, Marsala, and water to a boil, stirring to dissolve the sugar. Boil until a medium-thick, golden brown syrup forms, 3 to 5 minutes. Remove from the heat and add the figs, placing them cut side down. Let them soak for 15 or 20 minutes in the syrup, then turn and let them soak another 10 minutes.

While the figs are soaking, preheat an oven to 350°F. Butter a round baking dish that is at least 1

1/2 inches deep and 12 inches in diameter, or butter a rectangular dish measuring 12 inches by 18 inches.

To make the batter, combine in a mixing bowl the milk, 1/4 cup cream, brown sugar, eggs, vanilla, salt, and flour. Beat with an electric mixer until the mixture is frothy, about 5 minutes.

Pour enough of the batter into the prepared baking dish to cover the bottom with a layer about 1/4 inch deep. Put the dish in the preheated oven for 2 minutes. Remove the dish from the oven. Lift the figs from the syrup with a slotted spoon, reserving the syrup, and arrange the figs evenly over the batter. Vary the pattern, placing some figs cut side up and others cut side down. Pour the remaining batter over the figs.

Bake the *clafouti* in the preheated oven until puffed and brown and a knife inserted in the center comes out clean, 30 to 35 minutes.

Serve warm from the oven, plain or sprinkled with confectioners' sugar.

Serves 6 to 8

CHARENTAIS MELONS WITH PORT

Every summer an argument arises at tables all over France about whether or not filling the cavity of a Charentais melon with port or another fortified wine ruins or enhances the flavor of the melon. In my experience, any Charentais melon or very good cantaloupe, if it is a fraction less than perfectly ripe, is delicious with port or with another *vin doux*. If, on the other hand, you happen to have that rare and wonderful treat, a perfectly ripe melon, serve it *au natural*.

One Saturday I was a guest at the home of a French woman after we had gone shopping at the market in Apt. We were three people for lunch, and our hostess cut in half the three Charentais melons I had bought that morning. She filled the glowing orange cavities of three halves with an amber liquid and served each of us one of the halves. The liquid was a *vin doux maison* that she had made by adding fortified wine,

Charentais Melons with Port

sugar, and green walnuts, I think, to a local Luberon red wine. The melon and the *vin doux* in this case were made for each other and we each ate another wine-filled half.

2 CHARENTAIS MELONS OR CANTALOUPES
FRESH MINT LEAVES FOR GARNISH (OPTIONAL)
ABOUT 1 CUP PORT WINE

If the melons are chilling in the refrigerator, remove them 15 or 20 minutes before serving them. This will allow them to warm a bit, releasing the aroma and flavor. Picked in the garden or purchased from a farmers' or green market early in the morning, the melons can be left to stand in a cool place if they are to be eaten at lunch. Otherwise, the melons should be kept refrigerated, as they will continue to ripen past their prime when left at room temperature.

Cut the melons in half and scoop out and discard the seeds from the cavities. Put each half on a pretty dish, garnish with a sprig of mint, and fill the cavity to just below the brim with the port.

Serve either as dessert or as a first course.
Serves 4

COMPOTE OF PEACHES AND PLUMS

Peaches, plums, and nectarines all seem to ripen at once. When you have eaten your fill of fruits fresh off the trees, consider making a compote with them. Poach the firm, unblemished fruits in a wine syrup infused

Compote of Peaches and Plums with Wild Berry Tarts and Fresh Fig Clafouti

with vanilla just long enough to cook them through. Do not cook them too long or they will not hold their shape. The fruits can then be arranged in layers in a large, decorative glass jar with the rosy carmine syrup surrounding them.

Served from the jar, with a wedge of home-made pound cake or a scoop of vanilla ice cream, the compote is an elegant but homey dessert for a summer lunch or dinner. Eaten with buttered toast and coffee, the compote is also a sweet mid-morning treat.

The compote will keep for up to a week in the refrigerator.

2 CUPS DRY WHITE WINE

1 CUP WATER

1/2 CUP SUGAR

1 PIECE VANILLA BEAN (ABOUT
        6 INCHES LONG)

8 PEACHES (ABOUT 3 POUNDS), PEELED,
        HALVED, AND PITTED

12 TO 15 SMALL PLUMS (ABOUT 1 1/2
        POUNDS), HALVED AND PITTED

Combine the wine, water, sugar, and vanilla bean in a saucepan and bring to a boil, stirring to dissolve the sugar. Boil until a light syrup forms, 4 or 5 minutes.

Reduce the heat so that the syrup simmers gently and slip the peaches and plums into the pan. Poach the fruit for 5 minutes, then turn off the heat. Transfer the contents of the saucepan to a glass or enamel bowl. Let the fruit stand in the syrup until it is cool enough to handle. Using your fingers or a wooden spoon, carefully arrange the poached fruits in a pretty 2- to 3-quart glass jar that can act as a serving dish as well as a storage container. Pour the syrup over the arranged fruits.

The compote may be served warm or it may be covered, refrigerated, and served chilled.

Makes about 2 quarts; serves 8

WILD BERRY TARTS

Blackberries, bilberries, raspberries, blueberries, and boysenberries are a few of the berries that grow in almost every part of France and in the United States. They all make wonderful pies, jams, and tarts.

Tarts require the fewest berries and consequently I make those more frequently than pies or jams. It is easy to stop along a roadside for ten minutes and gather enough berries to make tarts for dinner, plus have a small bowl of berries leftover for breakfast the next day.

Tart Shells
2 CUPS ALL-PURPOSE FLOUR
1 TEASPOON SALT
1/2 CUP (1/4 POUND) UNSALTED BUTTER, CHILLED
3 TABLESPOONS MARGARINE, CHILLED
6 TABLESPOONS ICE WATER

Filling
1/3 CUP TART PLUM JELLY
1/4 CUP WATER
1/4 CUP SUGAR
2 CUPS BERRIES OF CHOICE

To make the tart shells, sift the flour and salt together into a bowl. Cut the butter and margarine into 1/2-inch chunks and add them to the flour mixture. With a pastry blender or 2 knives, cut in the butter and margarine until pea-sized balls form. Add the ice water, 1 tablespoon at a time. As you add the water, turn the dough with a fork and then with your fingertips. This will help to keep the pastry light and flaky. Do not overwork the dough or it will become tough. Gather the dough into a ball, wrap in plastic wrap or aluminum foil, and refrigerate it for 15 minutes. It will be easier to roll out if it is chilled.

Preheat an oven to 350°F. On a lightly floured work surface, roll out the dough 1/8 inch thick. Cut out 8 rounds, each 6 inches in diameter. (This is the size for 4-inch tart tins. If you are using tart pans of a different size, cut out rounds or other shapes 2 inches larger than the size of the pans.) Drape each round over the rolling pin and rest it on a tart pan. Unfold the dough and press it gently into the pan. Trim off the overlap even with the top of the pan. Mold the edges with the tines of a fork. Line each tart shell with aluminum foil. Add a layer of pastry weights or dried beans. Bake in the preheated oven 5 to 6 minutes. Remove from the oven and lift out the weights and foil. Prick each shell bottom with the tines of a fork to allow steam to escape. Return the pastry shells to the oven and bake until crisp and lightly browned, about 10 minutes longer. Remove the tart shells from the oven and let them cool completely.

While the tart shells are cooling, prepare the filling. Combine the jelly, water, sugar, and 1/2 of the berries in a saucepan. Bring to a boil, crushing the berries with the back of a fork as the mixture heats. Continue cooking the mixture until it is thick enough to coat the back of a spoon without dripping off, about 10 minutes. Remove from the heat and let cool until warm.

With a pastry brush, paint the bottom of each tart shell with some of the warm jelly mixture. Stack the berries as high as you dare in the tart shells and drizzle each with about 1 tablespoon of the jelly mixture. Serve warm or cold, in or out of the pans.

Makes eight 4-inch tarts; serves 8

F A L L

Cassoulet of Fresh Cranberry Beans, Duck, and Sausage (page 99)

FALL

The Crossover Season

The first days of fall are warm enough for the last of the summer fruits and vegetables to mature, yet cool enough to encourage leafy plant growth and the development of early roots. Plants grown from seeds sowed in late spring and early summer are yielding their first fruits, just in time to be harvested and stored for the coming winter, and late-season summer fruits and vegetables are at their sweetest. Twice-bearing fruit trees and vines are still in their second flush at the same time that a young, tender short-season crop of greens, lettuces, and roots are ready to harvest. Since fall fruits and vegetables share the characteristics of spring and summer ones and the weather has intimations of winter, even on hot, Indian summer days, it is a season that defies a rigid definition. In fact, it is the multifaceted nature of fall that I like so much, that makes it my favorite season.

A stroll through the markets will quickly verify the range of the season's traditional fruits and vegetables.

Displays of deep orange persimmons, red pomegranates, and flaming red Rouge d'Étampes and golden buff Musquée de Provence pumpkins are only a few feet away from equally impressive compositions of summer's red and yellow peppers, tomatoes, late-harvest melons, and scarlet pods of cranberry shell beans. Heads of tender lettuce, bundles of large-leaved chard, and curly green chicories are reminiscent of spring, as are the bunches of young turnips and carrots.

But the best of fall's traditional foods are, in my opinion, the wild mushrooms. I ate my first ones when I was living in Provence, and I have loved them ever since. Before that moment my ideas about wild mushrooms were typical of most Americans of the period who had been raised in an urban or suburban environment: all mushrooms except the white ones in the supermarket were probably poisonous toadstools. So when I met Victorine Frenet returning from a foray into the forest with a basket of what I thought were toadstools, I was both horrified and fascinated. She promptly pooh-poohed my ideas about toadstools and displayed the virtues of her finds, allowing me to examine the contents of her basket. Inside were about a dozen mushrooms with tan concave tops, marked with faint striations of brown. They had bits and pieces of pine needles and oak leaves stuck to them, and when Victorine broke one of the mushroom caps in half, it bled a red juice.

"They're called *sanguin*," Victorine explained, "because they bleed. The best way to cook them is on a grill, with a little garlic, salt, pepper, and olive oil. I'll show you tonight." She was right. They were earthy, meaty, rich, and unlike anything I had ever eaten before. I spent the next few weeks learning about where to find wild mushrooms and how to identify the good from the bad. I found chanterelles, cèpes, *sanguins*, puffballs, and lots of toadstools. I had a wonderful, wonderful time that year, and ever since I have looked forward to the first rains of fall, the signal that the wild mushroom season is beginning.

The fall *potager* is as diverse as the displays in the open markets. The light, bright greens of young chard, cabbages, new lettuces, and chicories contrast with the deep jewel tones of summer's last fruits and vegetables. Although the tomato vines are beginning to yellow and dry, they still hold ripe, golden, and scarlet fruits. Heavy clusters of magenta, honey gold, and indigo grapes hang amidst drying red and yellow leaves. In the late afternoon the slanting rays of the fall sun cast the garden in soft tones of mauve, salmon, gold, and lavender, spreading a warm glow over the red and yellow tomatoes, the orange persimmons, and the carmine-and-cream shell beans.

The culinary activities of the season parallel its disparate ingredients. In early fall look for simple salads of greens and young roots made from lettuce, arugula, turnips, and radishes that were planted in late summer.

As the season progresses, salads are more likely to combine frost-hardy greens and storage fruits with game birds and warm dressings.

I love the October smell of roasting chicken surrounded with turnips and carrots, wild mushrooms, and perhaps fennel and potatoes as well. Gratins of late leeks or early fennel served on chilly nights are something I begin looking forward to in August, when I am busy planting the seeds for my fall garden and pruning back the rampant summer herbs.

As I care for my summer garden, I also know that the flourishing basil will last into fall, when I can use it in a hearty beef daube thick with beans. As I clip rosemary for summer pizzas, I know that the resinous herb will still be growing strong in late October, for snipping to flavor roast fowl.

Fruits that grow throughout the summer but are harvested in late summer and early fall are the basis for the season's desserts. Big bowls piled high with persimmons, grapes, butter pears, and keeper apples are the classic end to a fall supper. For a more glamorous finale to a meal, fruits are poached in red wine and served in a pool of deep crimson syrup and rich cream.

Traditional fall fruits and vegetables are a study in different tastes, textures, and colors. Soft, juicy tomatoes and hard-shelled squashes and pumpkins are in the larder at the same time. Fresh green beans are blossoming for the last time in the garden, while the newly harvested shell beans are drying in the attic. Crunchy eighteen-day radishes can be eaten for lunch on the same day that parsnips and rutabagas, which have been growing for months, are dug up and put into storage. Hard-fleshed, knobby quinces and keeper apples fill my kitchen with their heavy aroma for a brief day or two before they go into storage to prepare for winter, which is on its way.

Classic Mesclun *Garden Salad*

CLASSIC *MESCLUN* GARDEN SALAD

At the marketplaces in and around Nice, almost every vendor of greens sells *mesclun* in addition to the usual lettuces, *frisées*, and escaroles. Literally translated as "mix" in the Niçoise dialect, *mesclun* is made up of many different young leaves, ranging from Merveille de Quatre Saisons lettuce to Fine de Louviers *frisée*, watercress, and *mâche*.

A traditional *potager,* especially in spring and fall, is full of young greens destined for *mesclun* salads.

One man, a native of Nice, gave me a list of what his grandmother said must be included in "true" *mesclun*.

In a delicate script she had written out twenty-one different items. Even for a typical *potager* in Nice, twenty-one greens is extensive. With a little preplanning and some careful seed ordering, however, anyone can have a salad garden in a small space that would be the equal of a French *mesclun* garden containing ten or twelve different greens. The mix can be whatever you would like, but for full effect the taste, texture, and color should be varied. Spicy arugula, tender lettuce leaves in different shades of green and red, pale lacy *frisée,* and several other varieties of chicories are the basics.

1 TEASPOON DIJON-STYLE MUSTARD
1/4 CUP COLD-PRESSED EXTRA-VIRGIN
    OLIVE OIL
2 TABLESPOONS BALSAMIC VINEGAR
1/8 TEASPOON SALT
1/4 TEASPOON FRESHLY GROUND BLACK PEPPER
4 CUPS MIXED LEAVES OF YOUNG LETTUCES,
    FRISÉE AND OTHER CHICORIES,
    AND ARUGULA

I usually make my dressing in the bottom of the salad bowl from which I am going to serve, then I add the greens and toss the salad at the table just before serving. Stir the mustard into the olive oil, then add the vinegar, salt, and pepper and mix well.

Pile the greens on top of the dressing and toss until the leaves are evenly coated.

Serves 4 to 6

Note: Mesclun salads are delicious topped with fresh goat cheese or homemade croutons (page 29).

SALAD OF SWEETBREADS, ARUGULA, AND RADISHES

This salad is full of straightforward taste sensations. Radishes and arugula share a strong, peppery taste, but one is eaten for its leafy tops and the other for its crunchy roots. They complement each other beautifully, and the unique taste of warm breaded sweetbreads dramatizes their flavors in the salad.

Sweetbreads need some preparation before they can be cooked. Cleaning them is a bit tedious, but well worth the effort. Plan on poaching the sweetbreads a day in advance and the salad will take only minutes to assemble and serve. If you are unable to get young, tender arugula, substitute a mixture of *radicchio*, spinach, and escarole or *frisée*.

Salad of Sweetbreads, Arugula, and Radishes

2 1/2 TO 3 POUNDS SWEETBREADS
3/4 CUP PLUS 2 TABLESPOONS FRESH LEMON
   JUICE OR DISTILLED WHITE VINEGAR

Dressing
1/4 CUP FRESH LEMON JUICE
1/4 CUP OLIVE OIL
1/2 TEASPOON SALT
1 TEASPOON FRESHLY GROUND BLACK PEPPER
1/2 TEASPOON PASILLA CHILI POWDER OR PAPRIKA

1/3 CUP HOMEMADE FINE DRIED BREAD CRUMBS
1/2 TEASPOON SALT
2 TEASPOONS FRESHLY GROUND BLACK PEPPER
1/2 TEASPOON DRIED THYME
2 EGGS
1/4 CUP VEGETABLE OIL, SUCH AS SAFFLOWER OIL
3 LARGE BUNCHES ARUGULA, TRIMMED AND TORN
   INTO BITE-SIZED PIECES (ABOUT 3 CUPS)
3 BUNCHES RADISHES (ABOUT 24 RADISHES),
   TRIMMED AND THINLY SLICED

Soak the sweetbreads in a large bowl of cold water to cover with 1/4 cup of the lemon juice or vinegar for 1 hour or so. Then, using your fingers, separate the lobes and remove the filmy white filaments. Repeat the soaking step twice, using fresh water and lemon juice or vinegar each time. Drain the sweetbreads and rinse them in clear water after the last soaking.

Place the sweetbreads in a large saucepan and add cold water to cover. Add the 2 tablespoons lemon juice or vinegar. Bring almost to a boil, reduce the heat, and poach for 15 minutes. Drain and cool to room temperature. The sweetbreads are now ready for breading or they may be covered and refrigerated for up to 36 hours.

Salad of Warm Duck, Lemons, and Kalamata Olives on a Bed of Fall Greens

To make the dressing, combine the lemon juice, olive oil, salt, pepper, and chili powder or paprika. Taste and adjust with salt, if necessary. Set aside.

To finish the sweetbreads, cut them into bite-sized slices. In a small, shallow bowl, mix together the bread crumbs, salt, pepper, and thyme. Break the eggs into a small bowl and beat lightly.

Heat the vegetable oil in a frying pan over high heat until it just begins to smoke. Reduce the heat to medium. A few at a time, dip the sweetbread slices into the beaten egg, then roll them in the seasoned bread crumbs. Add the slices to the pan and cook until golden brown, 1 or 2 minutes on each side. Remove to drain on paper towels and repeat until all the sweetbreads are cooked.

Combine the arugula and radishes in a large bowl. Add the warm sweetbreads and the dressing. Toss well and serve at once.

Serves 4 to 6

SALAD OF WARM DUCK, LEMONS, AND KALAMATA OLIVES ON A BED OF FALL GREENS

The Meyer lemons that grow beneath my kitchen window start ripening in late October, and from then on I am spoiled by an abundance of these tart, thin-skinned citrus fruits. I use the lemon juice in salad dressings, for poaching, and to season cooked greens, and I use cooked lemons as main ingredients.

In this warm salad, lemons are cut into small pieces and placed in the duck cavity, where they absorb the roasting juices and herbs as the bird cooks. They are then removed from the duck and used in the composed salad.

3 LEMONS, PREFERABLY MEYER VARIETY
1 DUCK (4 1/2 TO 5 POUNDS)
6 SPRIGS FRESH ROSEMARY
1 1/2 TEASPOONS SALT

1 1/2 TEASPOONS FRESHLY GROUND BLACK PEPPER

1 TABLESPOON OLIVE OIL

1 CLOVE GARLIC, CRUSHED

1/2 CUP DRY WHITE WINE

12 KALAMATA OLIVES

6 CUPS MIXED GREENS, SUCH AS
    RED MUSTARD, MIZUNA, ESCAROLE,
    FRISÉE, AND YOUNG KALE

Preheat an oven to 350°F. Cut 2 of the lemons into 1/2-inch-thick pieces and tuck the pieces into the duck's cavity. Reserve the other lemon to use in the dressing. Rub the outside of the duck with the rosemary and 1 teaspoon each of the salt and pepper. Roast the duck in the preheated oven until tender, about 1 1/2 hours. The skin should be crispy and the juice should run slightly pink when the thigh is pierced with the tip of a knife. When the duck is done, remove it from the oven and let it stand for 5 minutes. Remove the lemons from the cavity and set them aside. Slice the meat and keep it warm while you prepare the rest of the dish.

In a small saucepan or frying pan over medium heat, warm the olive oil. Add the garlic and sauté for 2 or 3 minutes. Add the wine and reduce the liquid over high heat by half. Add the juice of the reserved lemon, the olives, and the remaining 1/2 teaspoon each salt and pepper.

If the leaves of the greens are tender and small, leave them whole; if not, tear them into bite-sized pieces. Arrange the mixed greens on individual salad plates. Divide the cooked lemon pieces and the warm duck meat equally among them. I like the crispy duck skin in the salad, but you may prefer to remove it. Pour the warm dressing over the salads and serve immediately.

Serves 4 to 6

SAUTÉED GARLIC, RED PEPPERS, CHICORIES, CHARD, AND SPINACH FOR WHITE CHEDDAR POLENTA

Peppers, garlic, and greens are quickly sautéed in olive oil and then heaped onto a mound of creamy polenta, making a cheery, colorful dish. If you have greens growing in the garden, especially any chicories and dandelion that have become too strong to use raw in salads, this is the perfect way to serve them. Sautéing them in oil with garlic softens their bitterness, and they add an authentic taste to this rustic dish. I prepare this often, using odds and ends of garden greens. The simplicity of preparation belies a complex range of flavors.

Sautéed Garlic, Red Peppers, Chicories, Chard, and Spinach for White Cheddar Polenta

Polenta

6 CUPS WATER

1 TEASPOON SALT

1 CUP POLENTA

2 TABLESPOONS BUTTER

4 OUNCES WHITE CHEDDAR CHEESE, GRATED

1/2 TEASPOON SALT

1/2 TEASPOON FRESHLY GROUND BLACK PEPPER

Greens

1 BUNCH SWISS CHARD (10 TO 12 OUNCES),
     RIBS REMOVED

1 BUNCH CHICORY OR DANDELION GREENS
     (8 TO 10 OUNCES), STEMS REMOVED

1 BUNCH SPINACH (10 TO 12 OUNCES), TRIMMED

3 RED, GOLD, OR ORANGE BELL PEPPERS OR
     OTHER SWEET PEPPERS

2 TABLESPOONS OLIVE OIL

2 CLOVES GARLIC, CHOPPED

1/2 TEASPOON SALT

Pour the water into a saucepan, salt it, and bring it to a boil over high heat. Add the polenta in a very slow, steady stream, stirring as you pour. Reduce the heat and cook for 40 to 45 minutes, stirring frequently. The polenta is done when it pulls away slightly from the sides of the pan.

While the polenta is cooking, wash the greens carefully to remove any bits of sand or grit. With a sharp knife, cut the leaves lengthwise into 2 or 3 strips. Dry the greens thoroughly in a salad spinner or gather them up in a clean cloth and roll them dry.

Cut the peppers in half lengthwise and remove the seeds and ribs. Cut the halves lengthwise into thin slices.

Just before the polenta is ready, heat the olive oil in a large skillet and add the garlic and sweet peppers. Sauté for 2 or 3 minutes and then add the greens. Sprinkle with the salt, reduce the heat, cover the pan, and cook for 3 or 4 minutes. The greens will steam and reduce considerably in volume. Remove the cover and continue cooking until the greens are limp but still retain their color, a few minutes.

When the polenta is done, stir in the butter, cheese, salt, and pepper. Remove the pan from the heat and spread the polenta onto a warmed serving platter. Top it with the mixture of sautéed greens and peppers and serve at once.

Serves 4

CABBAGE LEAVES ROLLED WITH ROQUEFORT, PINE NUTS, AND *JAMBON CRU*

In late fall, when the cabbages have formed full, tight heads but are still mild and not yet musky with potent cabbage flavor, make these delicate cabbage rolls. Use the best *jambon cru* or prosciutto you can afford. You don't need much, and the taste of a good air-cured ham with the cheese and pine nuts makes an appetizer worthy of the season.

12 LARGE CABBAGE LEAVES

4 OUNCES ROQUEFORT OR OTHER BLUE CHEESE

2 TO 3 TABLESPOONS *MASCARPONE* CHEESE

1/8 TEASPOON SALT
1/4 TEASPOON FRESHLY GROUND BLACK PEPPER
1/4 CUP PINE NUTS, COARSELY CHOPPED
12 THIN SLICES *JAMBON CRU* OR PROSCIUTTO

Arrange the cabbage leaves on a large steamer rack over gently boiling water. Cover and steam until the leaves are limp, about 1 minute. Do not overcook. Immediately submerge the wilted leaves in cold water. Drain them and then gently dry; set aside.

In a small bowl combine the Roquefort and *mascarpone* cheeses, salt, and pepper; mix well. Cover

each leaf with a thin layer of the cheese mixture, spreading it to within 1/2 inch of the leaf edges. Sprinkle the pine nuts over the cheese. Place a slice of ham in the center of each leaf.

To form each roll, fold the bottom one-third of the thick stem end of each leaf over the filling. Fold in the sides of the leaves their entire length and then roll the leaf up. Cover and refrigerate the rolls until you are ready to serve them.

Makes 12 rolls; serves 6 to 12

Cabbage Leaves Rolled with Roquefort, Pine Nuts, and Jambon Cru

LEEK AND COD GRATIN

Salt cod is a common fall and winter ingredient in Provence, which is where I first ate it. On a very cold night, friends invited us over to celebrate their son's fifteenth birthday. The main dish was a golden-topped gratin made of tiny flakes of cod and sautéed leeks bound together in a delicate, creamy sauce. I had never tasted anything like it. I can still close my eyes and visualize the narrow wooden table running the length of the kitchen and the people sitting around it. And I remember exactly how the cod gratin tasted.

Salt cod is not commonly eaten in the United States outside of the Mediterranean and Caribbean communities, but I highly recommend discovering it. Its dense texture and fine flavor emerge after the fish has been refreshed for about a day in several changes of cold water.

1 POUND BONELESS SALT COD (SEE NOTE)
1 TABLESPOON OLIVE OIL
4 TABLESPOONS BUTTER
1 CUP MINCED LEEKS, INCLUDING SOME
    TENDER GREEN
2 TABLESPOONS ALL-PURPOSE FLOUR
1/4 TEASPOON SALT
1/2 TEASPOON FRESHLY GROUND BLACK PEPPER
1/4 TEASPOON CAYENNE PEPPER
3/4 CUP MILK
1/4 CUP FRESHLY GRATED GRUYÈRE CHEESE
2 TABLESPOONS CHOPPED FRESH PARSLEY
12 SALT-CURED BLACK OLIVES

Rinse the salt cod under running water for 10 minutes. Soak the salt cod in cold water to cover overnight. The next morning, change the water and let the cod stand covered for 4 hours. Change the water again and let

Leek and Cod Gratin

stand for another 2 hours. Rinse the cod under cold running water for 10 minutes. The cod will begin to plump up as it refreshes. Taste for saltiness. The actual length of time you will need to soak the cod will depend upon how much salt was used when it was cured. When desalted the taste will be mild and somewhat sweet.

Put the soaked cod in a shallow casserole or frying pan and add water to cover. Bring to a boil and reduce the heat to low. Cook just until the fish flakes when poked with a fork, 3 to 4 minutes. Remove from the water and let cool. When cool, separate into small flakes. If too salty, it may be rinsed again under cold running water. Be sure to squeeze all water from the flakes. They should be quite dry before adding them to the gratin. Set aside.

Heat the olive oil and 1 tablespoon of the butter in a skillet over medium heat. Add the leeks and sauté until they become translucent, about 5 minutes. Remove from the heat and set aside.

To make the sauce, melt 2 tablespoons of the butter in a heavy-bottomed saucepan over medium heat. When the butter begins to foam, remove the pan from the heat and whisk in the flour, salt, black pepper, and cayenne pepper until a paste forms. Return the pan to medium heat and gradually whisk in the milk in a steady stream. Reduce the heat to low and stir until there are no lumps. Simmer the sauce, stirring occasionally, until it becomes thick enough to coat the back of a spoon, about 10 minutes. Stir in the cheese and continue to cook only until the cheese has melted into the sauce, 2 or 3 minutes. Taste for seasonings and adjust for salt, if necessary.

Preheat an oven to 375°F. Combine the flaked cod, leeks and their cooking juices, the sauce, and the parsley. Butter an ovenproof dish just large enough to hold the mixture. Pour the cod mixture into the baking dish and dot with the olives. Cut the remaining tablespoon of butter into tiny bits and scatter the bits over the top. Bake in the preheated oven until a crisp, golden crust forms, 20 to 30 minutes.

Serves 4 to 6

Note: Good-quality cod is readily available in the meat and fish departments of well-stocked supermarkets, usually packed in little wooden boxes.

WHOLE ROAST FISH STUFFED WITH FENNEL

Fennel and fish are classic combinations in Provence. For the most typical preparations, the cavity of a full-bodied fish such as a dourade is filled with fennel leaves and then the fish is grilled on a bed of fennel branches over a grapevine fire. The flesh of the fish becomes delicately infused with the scent and taste of the fennel.

As a fennel lover, I have always felt a bit short-changed by the traditional method, and I prefer this version, which incorporates the fennel bulb as well as the leaves and branches or stalks. The vegetable fennel is a different variety than the herb fennel, which does not form a bulb. Generally fennel bulbs are sold with several inches of stalks attached and include some feathery leaves as well.

Although any type of fish may be used in this dish, inexpensive rock cod is an excellent choice. A three-pound rock cod has a good-sized cavity for stuffing and the sweet white flesh that flakes away easily from the bone is as succulent as you could wish for.

2 TO 3 MEDIUM-SIZED FENNEL BULBS
1/3 CUP FINE DRIED BREAD CRUMBS
JUICE OF 2 LIMES (ABOUT 1/4 CUP)
2 TABLESPOONS FINELY CHOPPED FRESH
  PARSLEY
1 TABLESPOON SALT
1 TABLESPOON FRESHLY GROUND BLACK PEPPER
1 WHOLE FISH (2 1/2 TO 3 POUNDS), SUCH AS
  ROCK COD OR SEA BASS, CLEANED
  WITH HEAD AND TAIL INTACT
2 TO 3 TABLESPOONS OLIVE OIL
2 TO 3 FENNEL BRANCHES (SEE NOTE)

Preheat an oven to 350°F. Trim away any brown or tough outer layers from the fennel bulbs. Cut off the leafy greens and the stalks. (Set these aside to use as the roasting bed if you do not have fennel branches.)

Mince the fennel bulbs and place them in a mixing bowl. Add the bread crumbs, lime juice, parsley, and 1/2 teaspoon each of the salt and pepper. Spoon as much of the fennel mixture into the cavity of the fish as it will hold. Sew the cavity closed with a needle and kitchen thread.

Rub the fish all over with the olive oil and the remaining 2 1/2 teaspoons each salt and pepper. Line the bottom of a large roasting pan with the fennel branches and put the fish on top. Roast the fish in the preheated oven for about 10 minutes per pound, or until the flesh bounces back when pressed. Another test

Whole Roast Fish Stuffed with Fennel

for doneness is to insert a sharp knife to the bone. If the flesh pulls away easily, the fish is done.

This whole fish ensures a dramatic presentation. I like to do all of the deboning at the table and not always without mishap. The end results are always satisfying, however.

To serve, first clip the thread of the sewn cavity and discard. Spoon the filling into a bowl to serve along with the fish. With a sharp knife make a cut along the backbone of the fish from head to tail. Make a crosscut

behind the head and another behind the tail. With the flat of the knife parallel to the bone, lift the meat away from the bone. Remove the bone by lifting the tail. The head will remain attached to the bone, leaving the other side of the fish neatly filleted.

Serves 5 or 6

Note: If you don't have long fennel branches, substitute the trimmed short stalks from the bulbs and 2 teaspoons fennel seed.

**GRILLED CHICKEN BREASTS ON CARROT
AND GREEN ONION *CONFITS***

Reduced to their essence with a bit of butter, olive oil, and sugar, carrots and green onions make simple *confits*. They can either be eaten on their own or used, as they are here, as a bed for grilled chicken breasts or other meats. The tarragon that seasons the chicken goes particularly well with the carrots and onions.

Marinade

2 TABLESPOONS CHOPPED FRESH TARRAGON

2 TABLESPOONS OLIVE OIL

1 TABLESPOON FRESH LEMON JUICE

1/4 TEASPOON SALT

1/4 TEASPOON FRESHLY GROUND BLACK PEPPER

4 WHOLE CHICKEN BREASTS, SKINNED,
        BONED, AND SPLIT

1 LARGE BUNCH CARROTS (ABOUT 12)

2 BUNCHES GREEN ONIONS (ABOUT 12)

2 TABLESPOONS BUTTER

4 TABLESPOONS OLIVE OIL

1 TABLESPOON SUGAR

SALT AND FRESHLY GROUND BLACK PEPPER TO TASTE

CARROT AND GREEN ONION SLIVERS FOR GARNISH

Mix all the marinade ingredients together in a small bowl. Arrange the chicken breasts in a shallow dish and brush them with the marinade. Set the chicken breasts aside while you prepare the vegetable *confits*.

Remove the carrot tops and cut the carrots into 1/4-inch-thick slices. Cut the onions into 1/4-inch-thick slices also, including 4 inches of the green tops.

Put 1 tablespoon of the butter and 2 table-spoons of the olive oil into a saucepan and heat them over medium heat until the butter melts. Add the carrots, turning them to coat well. At the same time, in a second pan melt the remaining 1 tablespoon butter with the remaining 2 tablespoons olive oil over medium heat. Add the onions, turning them to coat as you did the carrots. Reduce the heat to very low and cook until both the carrots and onions are very tender and soft but not mushy, 30 to 40 minutes. Add 1/2 tablespoon of the sugar to each pan and cook the carrots and onions until they begin to glisten and melt slightly, 5 to 10 minutes.

Meanwhile, prepare a fire in a charcoal grill or preheat a broiler. During the last 15 to 20 minutes that the *confits* are cooking, arrange the chicken breasts on a grill rack or a broiler pan and grill over a medium-hot fire or broil for 5 to 7 minutes on the first side. Turn the chicken breasts and cook 4 to 5 minutes longer.

To serve, warm the dinner plates. Spread half of each plate with a portion of carrot *confit*; spread the other half with a portion of the onion *confit*. Top each *confit* bed with a grilled chicken breast. Garnish the plates with carrot and onion slivers.

Serves 4

GARLIC-RUBBED ROAST CHICKEN WITH TURNIPS, CARROTS, AND WILD MUSHROOMS

A crisp roasted chicken, well rubbed with garlic and fresh herbs, is delicious on its own. Surrounded with savory roasted turnips and carrots and sautéed fall mushrooms, it becomes a feast. If you have your own herb garden or want to splurge in the market, stuff the cavity of the chicken with generous amounts of thyme and rosemary in addition to the herbs called for in the recipe.

1 CHICKEN (ABOUT 3 POUNDS), PREFERABLY WITH GIBLETS
1 TABLESPOON OLIVE OIL
4 CLOVES GARLIC, LIGHTLY CRUSHED
1 TEASPOON SALT
1 1/2 TABLESPOONS COARSELY GROUND BLACK PEPPER
2 TABLESPOONS CHOPPED FRESH ROSEMARY
5 TABLESPOONS CHOPPED FRESH THYME
6 TURNIPS, PEELED AND CUT INTO 6 PIECES
6 CARROTS, PEELED, HALVED, AND CUT INTO 3-INCH LENGTHS
8 TO 12 OUNCES MIXED FRESH WILD MUSHROOMS, SUCH AS CHANTERELLE, *SHIITAKE*, CÈPE, AND OYSTER, OR CULTIVATED BUTTON MUSHROOMS
1 TABLESPOON BUTTER

Preheat an oven to 350°F. If the chicken includes its giblets, set the liver, heart, gizzard, and neck aside. Rub the chicken with the olive oil and garlic, then put the spent garlic cloves in the chicken cavity.

In a small dish mix together the salt, pepper, rosemary, and thyme. Rub half of the mixture on the outside of the chicken. (If you have more thyme and rosemary, stuff them into the chicken cavity as described in the introduction.)

Put the chicken in a roasting dish large enough to hold it and the vegetables. Surround the chicken with the turnips and carrots. Add the reserved liver, heart, gizzard, and neck, if using. Sprinkle the vegetables and giblets with the remaining herb mixture. Roast the chicken and vegetables in the preheated oven, turning the vegetables from time to time to coat them with the pan juices. The chicken is done when it is crisp and golden and the tip of a sharp knife inserted into the thigh draws clear juice, 1 1/4 to 1 1/2 hours.

About 10 minutes before the chicken is done, prepare the mushrooms. Leave the mushrooms whole if possible, so they will not be lost among the larger carrots and turnips. If they are very large, halve them. In a sauté pan or skillet large enough to hold all the mushrooms, melt the butter over medium heat. When it foams, add the mushrooms and sauté, turning often, until just tender, 2 or 3 minutes. Add the hot mushrooms and their pan juices to the roast chicken and vegetables and serve immediately.

Serves 4 or 5

Garlic-Rubbed Roast Chicken with Turnips, Carrots, and Wild Mushrooms

CASSOULET OF FRESH CRANBERRY
BEANS, DUCK, AND SAUSAGE

Another of the great treats of late summer and early fall is fresh cranberry beans. For a brief period fresh beans are available in the markets, but the remainder of the year they can only be had dried. Variously called *cocos*, *borlotti*, or cranberry beans, depending upon whether you are in France, Italy, or the United States, the beans are about twice the size of kidney beans. Their background color ranges from brown to white and is always marked with reddish marbling of varying degrees. The pods are brilliant carmine and cream when fresh, turning to dusty violet and buff as they begin to dry.

    The cranberry taste is full of the flavor commonly associated with fresh green beans, but it is much meatier and richer. If fresh cranberry beans aren't in your market or garden, you can use other varieties of fresh shell beans, such as limas, kidneys, or *flageolets*.

    This cassoulet is not a classic version at all, but rather a mixture of some of the classic elements—beans, duck, and sausage—crowned with a nonclassical topping of garlicky bread crumbs and butter.

    I have especially fond memories of this dish. After a long day's drive in sheeting rain from the central French town of Le Puy to Aix-en-Provence in the south, my husband and I arrived late, tired, and very hungry on our friends' doorstep. We were greeted with a roaring oak fire, a glass of local red wine, and the aroma of this cassoulet, which tasted as good as it smelled.

3 SLICES BACON, CUT INTO 1/4-INCH PIECES
2 TABLESPOONS OLIVE OIL
2 CLOVES GARLIC, CHOPPED

1 LARGE OR 2 SMALL DUCKS (ABOUT 4 POUNDS TOTAL), CUT INTO SERVING PIECES
5 LARGE, VERY RIPE TOMATOES, PEELED AND COARSELY CHOPPED
2 TABLESPOONS CHOPPED FRESH THYME
1 TABLESPOON CHOPPED FRESH WINTER SAVORY
2 BAY LEAVES
4 CUPS FRESH SHELL BEANS, PREFERABLY CRANBERRY BEANS
4 MILD PORK SAUSAGES (EACH ABOUT 1 INCH THICK AND 4 INCHES LONG)

Topping
4 SLICES FRENCH BREAD, TOASTED
2 CLOVES GARLIC
1/4 TEASPOON SALT
1/2 TEASPOON MINCED FRESH THYME
1 TABLESPOON BUTTER

Preheat an oven to 325°F. In an ovenproof frying pan or flameproof casserole large enough to hold the beans and sausage as well as the duck, cook the bacon over low heat until it begins to release its fat, 3 or 4 minutes. Add the olive oil and increase the heat to medium. Add the garlic and sauté for 2 or 3 minutes. Add the duck pieces and sauté until lightly browned on all sides, 7 or 8 minutes. Add the tomatoes and herbs and mix well. Transfer the contents to an ovenproof dish if you are not using one already. Cover and cook in the preheated oven for 1 1/2 hours or longer. The cooking time will vary with the age and tenderness of the duck; wild ducks generally take longer to cook. The duck is ready when the meat easily pulls away from the bone. Remove the duck from the oven and increase the oven temperature to 400°F.

Add the shell beans and the sausages to the duck and enough water to cover the beans. Cook over medium-low heat until the beans are tender and the sausages are cooked through, 20 to 30 minutes. Stir occasionally during cooking.

To make the topping, grate the bread in a clean, dry blender or by hand. Grate the garlic. In a bowl, mix together the crumbs, garlic, salt, and thyme. Sprinkle the casserole with the crumb mixture. Cut the butter into bits and dot the casserole with the bits. Place the casserole in the oven to brown, about 10 minutes.

Serves 6 to 8

BEEF AND BASIL DAUBE WITH FLAGEOLETS AND HARICOTS VERTS

This rich stew incorporates the best of the early fall garden. Tomatoes, basil, and green beans are at the final peak of flavor before fall frosts chill them, and the pods of the *flageolet* shell beans have just started to plump and fill. The meat cooks slowly with herbs, while the beans are steamed separately and then added during the final stages of cooking, along with a creamy basil sauce. A mixture of bread crumbs, herbs, and garlic forms the golden crust.

2 1/2 TO 3 POUNDS BONELESS CHUCK, CUT
    INTO 2-INCH CUBES
3 TABLESPOONS ALL-PURPOSE FLOUR
1 TABLESPOON OLIVE OIL
2 ONIONS, CHOPPED
2 CLOVES GARLIC, CHOPPED
1 CUP DRY RED WINE
8 LARGE, VERY RIPE TOMATOES, PEELED
    AND CHOPPED
1 CUP BEEF STOCK
1 1/2 CUPS SHELLED FRESH *FLAGEOLET* OR LIMA
    BEANS (ABOUT 2 POUNDS UNSHELLED), OR
    3/4 CUP DRIED *FLAGEOLET* OR LIMA BEANS
1 POUND *HARICOTS VERTS* OR VERY YOUNG
    BLUE LAKE BEANS (SEE NOTE)

Basil Sauce
18 LARGE FRESH BASIL LEAVES
1/4 CUP OLIVE OIL
1 TABLESPOON FRESH THYME LEAVES
1/4 TEASPOON SALT

Fall Haricots Verts

Topping
4 SLICES DRY FRENCH BREAD
3 CLOVES GARLIC, CHOPPED
12 LARGE FRESH BASIL LEAVES, CHOPPED
1/4 TEASPOON SALT
1/2 TEASPOON FRESHLY GROUND BLACK PEPPER

1 TABLESPOON BUTTER
1 SPRIG FRESH BASIL

Roll the beef cubes in the flour until they are well coated. In a heavy-bottomed flameproof casserole or dutch oven large enough to hold the stew eventually, heat the olive oil over medium heat. Add the onions and garlic and sauté for about 5 minutes. Add the floured meat and cook, turning occasionally, until browned on all sides, 10 to 15 minutes. Add the wine and cook for 3 or 4 minutes, stirring constantly and scraping up any bits that have clung to the bottom of the pan. Add the tomatoes and beef stock, cover, and simmer until the beef is tender, 2 1/2 to 3 hours.

While the meat is cooking, prepare the beans. If using fresh *flageolet* or lima beans, arrange them on a steamer rack over gently boiling water. Cover and steam until tender, about 20 minutes. If using dried beans, simmer them in a generous amount of salted water until they are tender but not mushy. Allow 1 to 1 1/2 hours for the dried lima beans, and up to 2 hours longer for the dried *flageolet* beans. Drain well.

Arrange the *haricots verts* or Blue Lake beans on a steamer rack over gently boiling water. Cover and steam until just barely tender and still bright green, 2 or 3 minutes. Rinse them under cold water and set them aside.

To make the sauce, combine all of the ingredients in a blender and purée them. Alternatively, finely

Beef and Basil Daube with Flageolets *and* Haricots Verts

chop the basil and thyme and whisk them together with the oil and salt. Set the sauce aside.

To make the topping, grate the bread slices in a clean, dry blender or by hand. Stir in the garlic, salt, pepper, and, finally, the basil leaves. Set aside.

Preheat an oven to 450°F. Remove the beef from the stove. Transfer the beef to an ovenproof casserole if it is not already in an ovenproof vessel. Stir in the cooked *flageolet* or lima beans, the basil sauce, and three-fourths of the green beans. Strew the topping over the surface. Cut the butter into small bits and dot the casserole with the bits.

Bake the daube in the preheated oven until the top is golden brown, 8 to 10 minutes. Remove the daube from the oven and garnish the top with the reserved green beans. Break the crust a bit to allow the juices to come through. Tuck a sprig of basil into the edge of the dish and serve.

Serves 6 to 8

Note: Haricots verts are very quick and easy to grow and many different varieties are available through mail-order seed catalogs. If you do not grow them in your garden and cannot find them in the market, substitute very small, very fresh Blue Lake beans. The pods of most other green beans are too heavy for this dish.

SANDWICHES OF GREEN-SHOULDERED TOMATOES

Certain European tomato varieties have green shoulders when fully ripe, as do many American heirloom varieties. Green-shouldered types are firm, on the acidic side, and soak up marinades, which makes them perfect for sandwiches. In this sandwich, marinated tomatoes and fresh basil leaves are slipped between slices of cheese-filled bread that have been grilled in butter until the cheese begins to melt. If you can't find a true green-shouldered type, try underripe red tomatoes.

1/2 CUP COLD-PRESSED EXTRA-VIRGIN OLIVE OIL
4 CLOVES GARLIC, CRUSHED AND CHOPPED
1 SMALL, DRIED RED CHILI PEPPER
1 TEASPOON WHOLE BLACK PEPPERCORNS
1/4 TEASPOON SALT
4 OR 5 GREEN-SHOULDERED TOMATOES, SLICED 1/3 INCH THICK
8 LARGE, THICK SLICES SOURDOUGH BREAD OR *FOCACCIA*
2 TABLESPOONS BUTTER
2 TO 3 OUNCES FONTINA CHEESE, SLICED
12 TO 16 FRESH BASIL LEAVES

In a large, shallow dish, combine the olive oil, garlic, chili pepper, peppercorns, and salt; mix well. Add the tomatoes and let them stand in the oil mixture at room temperature for at least 6 hours.

Brush one side of each bread slice with some of the marinade mixture. Distribute the Fontina cheese evenly among half of the bread slices, placing the cheese on the oil-brushed sides. Top the cheese with a second bread slice, oiled side in, to make 4 sandwiches in all.

Sandwiches of Green-Shouldered Tomatoes

In a frying pan large enough to hold all of the sandwiches at one time, melt the butter over low heat. Add the sandwiches and cook, turning once, until they are golden brown on both sides and the cheese melts, 7 or 8 minutes. Remove the pan from the heat.

Tuck some of the tomato slices and 3 or 4 basil leaves into each sandwich. Serve hot.

Serves 4

END-OF-SEASON TOMATO *Coulis* FOR PASTA

I once spent an Indian summer month at the farmhouse of French friends in the countryside near Aix-en-Provence. Sweet, ripe tomatoes were everywhere and we cooked pounds and pounds of them down into a thick *coulis*. The tomatoes were so full of sugar and flavor, we added only a little garlic and salt. All month long we kept the refrigerator stocked with the fresh tomato sauce. We used it mostly for pasta and sometimes for pizza topping and for adding to stews. If the tomatoes are less than perfectly sweet, add a little sugar. Should you have truly sweet tomatoes, however, you won't need any.

2 TABLESPOONS OLIVE OIL

1 CLOVE GARLIC, CRUSHED AND MINCED

5 POUNDS VERY RIPE TOMATOES, PEELED

1/2 TEASPOON SALT

1/2 TEASPOON FRESHLY GROUND BLACK PEPPER

1/2 TO 1 TABLESPOON SUGAR (OPTIONAL)

1 TABLESPOON MINCED FRESH THYME

Heat the olive oil in a saucepan or frying pan large enough to hold all the tomatoes at one time. Add the garlic and sauté for 2 or 3 minutes, being careful not to brown it. Add the tomatoes and cook over low heat for 30 minutes.

Taste the sauce and add the salt, pepper, and the sugar, if needed. Continue cooking until the sauce thickens, another 30 minutes to 1 hour, depending upon the type of tomato. Skim any remaining clear liquid off the sauce. Stir in the thyme and cook for another 10 minutes.

Let the *coulis* cool, then bottle it and keep it refrigerated. In France, *coulis* is usually stored in wine bottles with corks. You just pull out the cork, shake a little sauce onto the hot pasta, and serve.

Makes about 3 cups

LATE SUMMER PEARS POACHED IN YOUNG WINE

For me, this is a perfect fall dessert. It combines sunny memories of summer with the promise of cozy fireside winter days. A young, slightly rough wine like a Cahors from southwest France is perfect for the poaching, but a similar California wine is equally good.

Look for pears that ripen late in the season, such as Boscs or Red Bartletts. These are good choices because they are generally firmer than the earlier ripening varieties and will hold their shape during poaching.

Heavy cream mixed with rosemary and a tiny bit of freshly ground black pepper accentuate the flavor of the wine-poached pears.

4 PEARS
1 1/2 CUPS RED WINE
2 TABLESPOONS SUGAR
1/2 CUP HEAVY CREAM
2 TABLESPOONS FINELY CHOPPED FRESH ROSEMARY

Halve the pears lengthwise, leaving the stem intact on one half. Scoop out and discard the seeds. Remove the string that runs down the center from the stem end to the seed cavity. You may peel the pears or leave them unpeeled. I think keeping the golden green skin on half of the pears and peeling the skins from the remaining halves makes a pretty presentation.

In a skillet or saucepan large enough to hold all the pear halves in a single layer, bring the wine and 1 tablespoon of the sugar to a boil, stirring to dissolve the sugar. Cook over high heat for 3 or 4 minutes. Reduce the heat, add the pears, and poach until just tender, 15 to 20 minutes. Do not overcook the pears or they will become mushy.

Transfer the pears and the poaching liquid to a glass or ceramic bowl and let stand for several hours at room temperature. Turn the pears from time to time. They will become a beautiful, deep garnet color as they absorb the wine.

In a small bowl, mix the cream, the remaining 1 tablespoon of sugar, and the rosemary together. To serve the pears, put a few spoonfuls of the cream mixture onto each dessert plate. Add a pear half and a single spoonful of the poaching liquid.

Serves 6 to 8

PERSIMMON FLAN

Adding puréed persimmon to the custard mixture changes the color, taste, and texture of the classic flan. The egg custard takes on a golden hue, and sweet, puréed persimmon sinks into the caramelized sugar in the bottom of the baking dish and becomes part of the topping when the flan is inverted onto a serving plate.

When choosing persimmons, look for the Hachiya variety. The nonstem end is pointed rather than flat like that of the Fuyu variety. When it is perfectly ripe, the Hachiya is burnt orange red, very soft, and purées beautifully. In contrast, the Fuyu is light orange and is quite firm even when ripe and sweet.

This dessert is delicious warm, but may also be served chilled.

Late Summer Pears Poached in Young Wine

1 CUP SUGAR

2 OR 3 VERY RIPE PERSIMMONS, PREFERABLY
 HACHIYA VARIETY

1 CUP MILK

2 CUPS HEAVY CREAM

6 EGGS

1/2 TEASPOON SALT

1 TEASPOON VANILLA EXTRACT

To make the caramel that will eventually be the topping on the flan, put 1/2 cup of the sugar in an 8-inch cake pan and heat it on top of the stove over medium-low heat. Holding the edge of the pan with a hot pad, tilt the pan from side to side as the sugar melts and caramelizes. When all the sugar has melted into a dark brown liquid, remove the pan from the stove. Tip the pan so that the sides as well as the bottom are coated with the syrup. Set the pan aside.

Peel and seed the persimmons, then cut them into chunks. Place them in a small saucepan and cook them over medium heat for 5 minutes, stirring often. Purée the fruit in a blender, then strain it through a wire-mesh sieve. You should have about 3/4 cup thick purée. Discard any fibers in the strainer and set the purée aside.

Preheat an oven to 325°F. Heat the milk and cream together in a saucepan over medium heat until bubbles form around the edges. At the same time, put on a kettle of water and bring it to a boil.

In a bowl beat the eggs lightly and then add the remaining 1/2 cup sugar, the salt, and vanilla. When the milk-cream mixture is ready, slowly pour it into the egg mixture, stirring continuously. Stir in the puréed fruit.

Put the caramelized cake pan in a shallow roasting pan large enough to hold it. Pour the custard into the cake pan; it should fill it to the rim. Pour the boiling water into the roasting pan until it reaches halfway up the sides of the cake pan.

Bake the custard in the preheated oven until a knife inserted into the middle of the flan comes out clean, 35 to 45 minutes.

Remove the flan from the oven and let it cool to room temperature. At this point it can be served, or it can be refrigerated for several hours.

To unmold the flan, slide a thin-bladed knife or spatula around the edge of the pan to loosen it. Invert a shallow serving plate on top of the flan and, holding the flan and the serving plate firmly together, flip them. The flan pan will now be on top and should lift off. If the flan didn't unmold on the flip, give the pan a shake to encourage it.

Makes 8 to 10 servings

Persimmon Flan

WINTER

Salad of Orange, Fennel, Red Onion, and Green Olives (page 112)

WINTER

The Dormant Season

Winter days are short and cold, causing plant growth to cease. Traditional seasonal vegetables and fruits are either those that have already been harvested and stored or those few that can stay in the field or garden relatively undamaged by frosts. These are complemented in the kitchen by winter citrus fruits.

Harvested fruits and vegetables can be stored over winter in a number of ways. Perishable summer stone fruits can be dried, packed into sweetened alcohol syrups, or cooked into preserves or jellies. The pome fruits—apples, pears, and quinces—from late summer and early fall harvests will keep for several months in a cool, dark, well-ventilated place, as will hard squashes and winter roots. Onions and potatoes dug in fall and properly stored will keep until spring. Brine- or salt-cured olives and a variety of nuts and dried beans make up the remainder of a traditional winter larder.

Although the kitchen garden is at its sparest in the winter months, in all but the most severe climates it still supplies leeks; hardy winter greens such as kale, cabbage, *radicchio*, and chicories; and parsley and chervil. From the market vendors come parsnips, rutabagas, turnips, winter carrots, storage potatoes and onions, celery root, fennel, winter greens—escarole, *frisée*, and Belgian endive—and oranges and lemons.

Winter dishes are full of strong tastes. For fresh salads the season gives us peppery watercress, slightly bitter Belgian endive, and *radicchio* leaves. Or there is crunchy raw fennel tasting like licorice-flavored celery for combining with tart citrus or with the cream-colored, somewhat bitter leaves of escarole and *frisée*. From storage come salt-cured olives, resinous pine nuts, and toasted almonds, all assertively flavored additions to winter salads.

The seasonal soups, stews, and gratins use many of the same ingredients as the salads. Gratins of Belgian endive, fennel, chard, or other greens are liberally laced with creamy sauces before going under the broiler. Kale and cabbage are slowly cooked in soups, along with dried beans or maybe winter squashes. Caramelized onions and shallots, grilled *radicchio*, and roasted fennel are all good winter accompaniments for meats; they also make substantial toppings and fillings for breads and for rolled vegetable leaves or thin pancakes. Pungent celery roots and sweet parsnips make equally delicious roasted chips, good choices for serving with stews or roasts.

Salty anchovies and olives from the larder go surprisingly well with winter's starchy potatoes and storage onions. All kinds of dried beans are good in slow-simmered dishes, especially if the beans were harvested the preceding fall and still retain their fresh flavor.

Desserts depend on fruits that can keep well in cold-weather storage conditions, such as apples and quinces. These hardy fruits are made into pies, tarts, sauces, compotes, creams, and puddings. Dried raisins and figs from the fall harvest, nuts of all kinds, and the juice and zest of oranges and lemons infuse fruit desserts with flavor. Almonds make delicious pastries and creams on their own, as do lemons. Preserves made during spring, summer, and fall are important to the winter dessert menu. Cherries, grapes, and tiny plums that have been soaking in brandy or Armagnac for several months make perfect toppings for pound cake or ice cream, or are good on their own with a cookie or two. For a special occasion, the brandy-soaked fruits and their juices can be turned into jewel-toned sorbets.

Obviously no other season relies as heavily on stored and preserved foods from other seasons, but great variety still exists. Daily trips to a *potager* always produce some fresh greens and a handful of other vegetables. As has been noted, potatoes, onions, winter squashes, and roots of all kinds are the standard vegetables; apples, quinces, winter pears, and citrus are the common fruits.

In addition, the shelves of the well-stocked winter kitchen always hold a jar or two of preserved fruits, some pickled mushrooms, a storehouse of special muscat grapes dried into plump golden raisins, homemade fruit syrups, and all kinds of olives, nuts, and dried beans.

Salad of Orange, Fennel, Red Onion, and Green Olives

Fennel, also called sweet anise and *finocchio*, is an underestimated vegetable in this country and merits wider usage. Crisp and succulent like celery, but with a slightly licorice flavor, fennel is a fine partner to most fruits and greens. It also goes well with robust ingredients such as salt-cured olives and sharp, dry cheeses. Fennel may be used raw, as in this composed winter salad, or cooked and served as a vegetable.

Dressing
Juice of 2 lemons (about 6 tablespoons)
1 tablespoon finely chopped fennel leaves
2 tablespoons chopped fresh chervil
2 tablespoons heavy cream
1/2 teaspoon salt
1/2 teaspoon freshly ground black pepper

1 large fennel bulb
1/2 red onion (cut stem to root)
2 oranges

1 CUP TORN MIXED GREENS, SUCH AS
   WATERCRESS, ARUGULA, AND YOUNG
   LETTUCES
12 TO 16 BRIGHT GREEN GREEK OR
   ITALIAN OLIVES
1 TABLESPOON FINELY CHOPPED FENNEL
   LEAVES FOR GARNISH

In a small bowl, combine all the ingredients for the dressing and let stand for 1 to 2 hours at room tem-

perature to allow the flavors to blend.

Trim away the top of the fennel bulb and remove any brown or tough outer layers. Cut the fennel into julienne strips and place in a glass bowl. Cut the onion lengthwise into thin slices and add it to the bowl with the fennel. Cut 1 orange in half crosswise. Squeeze the juice from one-half and add it to the bowl. Turn the fennel strips and onion slices, coating them with the juice. Let stand for 1 hour at room temperature.

Remove the zest from the remaining 1 1/2

oranges and slice it into thin slivers; set aside. Cut the oranges crosswise into 1/4-inch-thick slices. Remove any seeds and trim away the white pith. Refrigerate the slices until you are ready to assemble the salads.

To assemble the salads, arrange a bed of mixed greens on each plate and top with the fennel and onion. Place the orange slices on top. Drizzle each salad with some of the dressing. Garnish with the olives, orange zest, and fennel leaves.

Serves 4

POACHED RED TROUT, BELGIAN ENDIVE, AND WATERCRESS SALAD

In winter red, or salmon, trout are available in the fish markets, and I buy them often because I like how they combine a salmonlike taste and color with the naturally delicate flesh of trout. Browned in butter and then poached in tarragon-flavored white wine, these mild fish render a broth that forms part of the salad dressing.

Poached Red Trout, Belgian Endive, and Watercress Salad

Any greens can be used for the salad, but I think peppery watercress and crisp, slightly bitter Belgian endive go especially well with the citrus and tarragon flavors of the dressing.

1 BUNCH WATERCRESS

2 HEADS BELGIAN ENDIVE

1 TABLESPOON BUTTER

1 TABLESPOON CHOPPED SHALLOTS

1 WHOLE RED TROUT (ABOUT 1 POUND), CLEANED, OR 2 OR 3 RED TROUT FILLETS (8 TO 12 OUNCES TOTAL WEIGHT)

SALT TO TASTE, PLUS 1/8 TEASPOON SALT

FRESHLY GROUND BLACK PEPPER TO TASTE

4 TABLESPOONS FRESH TARRAGON LEAVES

1/2 CUP DRY WHITE WINE

2 TABLESPOONS FRESH LEMON JUICE

2 TO 3 TABLESPOONS OLIVE OIL (OPTIONAL)

Choose 4 delicate clusters of watercress and reserve these to garnish the plates. Remove the leaves from the remaining watercress and set the leaves aside. Cut out the inverted V-shaped cores of the Belgian endives with a small, sharp knife. Separate the endive leaves and set aside 12 small, beautiful ones. Chop the remaining Belgian endive leaves and refrigerate, along with the watercress.

In a skillet large enough to hold the trout, melt the butter over medium heat. Add the shallots and sauté for 2 to 3 minutes. Season the trout with salt and pepper to taste. If using a whole fish, tuck 1 tablespoon of the tarragon leaves into the cavity; if using fillets sprinkle the leaves on top. Put the trout into the pan (skin side down, if using fillets) and cook 2 to 3 min-

utes. If using a whole trout, turn and cook 2 to 3 minutes on the second side. Add 1/4 cup of the wine, reduce the heat to low, and cover the pan. Cook until the fish is just done, 3 to 4 minutes. Remove the fish from the pan and set it aside while you prepare the dressing.

To the cooking juices that remain in the skillet, add the remaining 3 tablespoons tarragon leaves, the lemon juice, 1/8 teaspoon salt, and the remaining 1/4 cup wine. Bring to a boil over medium-high heat and reduce by half. Taste and correct the seasoning. If the dressing seems too tart, add 2 to 3 tablespoons olive oil to smooth it out. Pour the dressing into a small bowl and set aside.

To serve the salad, flake the trout flesh into large pieces. Divide the chopped endive among 4 salad plates. Add an equal amount of watercress leaves and flaked trout to each plate. Garnish with the reserved watercress clusters and the whole endive leaves. Drizzle some of the dressing over each plate and serve at once.

Serves 4

PISSALADIÈRE WITH CARAMELIZED ONIONS, NIÇOISE OLIVES, AND FRESH OREGANO

Pissaladière is the pizza of the Provence. It is especially popular in the areas around Nice and Marseilles. Baked in a shallow, rectangular pan, *pissaladière* is traditionally cut into large squares and served at room temperature. The topping is usually olive oil, a thin layer of dense

Pissaladière *with Caramelized Onions, Niçoise Olives, and Fresh Oregano*

tomato sauce, salt-cured black olives, and anchovies. In this more unusual version, a thick layer of caramelized onions replaces the tomato and lots of fresh oregano is used as well.

Crust

2 ENVELOPES (SCANT 1 TABLESPOON EACH)
    ACTIVE DRY YEAST
1 CUP WARM WATER (105°F)
1 TEASPOON SUGAR
1 TEASPOON SALT
3 1/2 CUPS ALL-PURPOSE FLOUR
CORNMEAL FOR PAN

Topping

8 TABLESPOONS OLIVE OIL
4 TABLESPOONS BUTTER
15 ONIONS (ABOUT 5 POUNDS), THINLY SLICED
4 BAY LEAVES
1 TABLESPOON SUGAR
1 TEASPOON SALT
2 TABLESPOONS DRY WHITE WINE
1/4 CUP FRESH OREGANO OR MARJORAM
    LEAVES, FINELY CHOPPED
1/4 CUP FRESHLY GRATED ASIAGO OR
    PARMESAN CHEESE
12 NIÇOISE OLIVES

The dough is quickly made in a food processor or can be made by hand. In a small bowl dissolve the yeast in the warm water. Add the sugar and let stand until foamy, about 5 minutes. In a food processor bowl fitted with a metal blade, combine the yeast mixture, salt, and 1 3/4 cups of the flour. Process 3 to 4 minutes. Add the remaining 1 3/4 cups flour and process until the dough forms a ball, about 2 minutes. If preparing the dough by hand, follow the same steps, combining all the ingredients in a large bowl and mixing with a fork or your fingertips until the dough forms a ball. When the dough ball is formed, either in the food processor or by hand, turn it out onto a lightly floured surface and knead until the dough is elastic, 6 or 7 minutes.

Gather the dough into a smooth ball and place it in a lightly oiled bowl. Turn the ball to coat the surface evenly with the oil. Cover the bowl with a clean cloth and place in a warm place to rise for 1 hour.

Meanwhile, make the topping. Combine 6 tablespoons of the olive oil and the butter in a large, heavy-bottomed saucepan over medium heat. When the butter foams, add half of the sliced onions and 2 of the bay leaves. Sprinkle with 1/2 tablespoon of the sugar and 1/2 teaspoon of the salt. Add the remaining sliced onions and top with the remaining sugar, salt, and bay leaves. Cover, reduce the heat to low, and cook for 20 minutes. Remove the lid, stir the onions, and increase the heat to medium. Cook for another 15 minutes, stirring occasionally. Finally, increase the heat to high and cook, stirring constantly until the onions are a deep golden brown, about 10 minutes. Add the wine and stir well to dislodge any browned bits stuck to the pan bottom. Cook for 5 or 6 minutes, then remove the pan from the heat and set aside.

Preheat the oven to 500°F. Punch down the dough in the bowl, re-cover it with the cloth, and let it rest for 15 minutes.

On a lightly floured board, roll out the dough to fit a 20-by-30-by-1-inch baking sheet. Sprinkle the baking sheet lightly with the cornmeal. Drape the dough over the rolling pin and transfer it to the prepared baking sheet. Unfold the dough and gently press it into the pan, rolling the edges outward to form a rim. Drizzle the surface with 1 tablespoon of the remaining olive oil. Remove and discard the bay leaves and then spread the onions evenly over the surface of the dough. Sprinkle with the cheese and add the olives, spacing them evenly. Bake in the preheated oven until the crust is golden and crispy, 12 to 15 minutes.

Remove the *pissaladière* from the oven and immediately drizzle the remaining 1 tablespoon olive oil over the top. Sprinkle it evenly with the oregano or marjoram. Cut into 12 squares and serve hot or at room temperature.

Serves 8 to 12 as a first course, or 4 to 6 as a main course

DEEP-DISH BLACK CABBAGE
AND BEAN SOUP
WITH ANCHOVY CRUST

Black cabbage is not a cabbage at all, but a variety of kale. It resembles a Savoy cabbage gone primitive, one in which the leaves have grown tall and wide instead of close and cupping. It has a wonderful thick texture and a fine, sweet flavor, especially after a hard frost. If you can get it, use it by all means, but any other kale is a good substitute.

This is a hearty and satisfying soup that can be served as a first course or a meal in itself. The beans are cooked separately, then combined with the cabbage and stock. A biscuitlike dough flavored with thyme and anchovies covers the finished soup and is baked to a fragrant browned crust.

1 CUP DRIED CRANBERRY BEANS OR OTHER
    LARGE, MEATY DRIED BEANS
8 TO 10 CUPS WATER
SALT
2 BUNCHES BLACK CABBAGE OR OTHER KALE,
    THICK RIBS REMOVED
6 CUPS CHICKEN STOCK
2 TABLESPOONS OLIVE OIL
1/4 CUP CHOPPED ONION
4 CLOVES GARLIC, CHOPPED
2 SLICES *PANCETTA* OR SMOKED BACON,
    CHOPPED
2 POTATOES, PEELED AND DICED
BOUQUET GARNI OF 4 SPRIGS FRESH THYME
    AND 3 SPRIGS FRESH PARSLEY

Anchovy Crust
2 CUPS ALL-PURPOSE FLOUR
1 TABLESPOON BAKING POWDER
1/2 TEASPOON SALT
1/3 CUP SOLID VEGETABLE SHORTENING,
    BUTTER, OR MARGARINE, CUT
    INTO 1/2-INCH CHUNKS
1 CAN (2 OUNCES) FLAT ANCHOVY FILLETS
    IN OIL, DRAINED AND FINELY
    CHOPPED
1/4 CUP CHOPPED FRESH THYME
3/4 TO 7/8 CUP MILK
1 TABLESPOON BUTTER, MELTED

fourths of the liquid. Return about one fourth of the beans to the liquid and, with the back of a wooden spoon, mash the beans to thicken the liquid. Reserve the beans and the bean liquid. This step can be done a day ahead, if desired.

In a saucepan simmer the cabbage in the chicken stock until tender, about 45 minutes. Using a slotted spoon, remove the cabbage from the stock. Reserve the stock. Squeeze as much liquid as possible from the cabbage. Chop the cabbage, removing and discarding any coarse bits of stem.

In a deep, heavy-bottomed soup pot, heat the olive oil over medium heat. Add the onion, garlic, and *pancetta* and sauté lightly for a few minutes. Add the reserved stock, chopped cabbage, cooked beans, thickened bean liquid, and potatoes. Tie the thyme sprigs and parsley sprigs in a bouquet garni and add to the pot. Simmer for 30 minutes.

While the soup is simmering, make the crust. Combine the flour, baking powder, and salt in a bowl. Cut in the shortening with a pastry blender or 2 knives until the mixture is the texture of cornmeal. Add the anchovies and thyme and mix lightly. Dribble in 3/4 cup milk, tossing with a fork until evenly moistened. Gather the dough into a ball. If it feels too dry, add a little more milk. Place the dough ball on a lightly floured board and knead until it is well blended but sticky, about 1 minute. Let the dough stand for a few minutes before rolling it out.

Preheat an oven to 425°F. Choose a deep oven-proof dish 10 to 12 inches in diameter that can go directly to the table. Pour the hot soup into the dish, discarding the bouquet garni. On the lightly floured board, pat or roll out the dough 1/2 inch thick into a shape large enough to cover the dish. Drape it around

Place the beans in a bowl and add water to cover generously. Let soak overnight. The next day, drain the beans and place them in a saucepan. Add the water, bring to a boil, reduce the heat, and simmer, covered, until tender. This will take 2 to 3 hours, depending upon the type and age of the dried beans. During the cooking, salt the beans well; if they are cooked in unsalted water they will taste bland. When the beans are soft throughout, turn off the heat and allow them to cool down in the cooking liquid. Strain the beans and reserve three

the rolling pin and transfer it to the baking dish. Unfold it and stretch it across the dish so that it just hangs over the edge, or lay it directly on the surface of the soup. Either way works well. Brush the dough with the melted butter. Bake the soup in the preheated oven until the crust is nicely browned, 20 to 25 minutes.

Serve hot. Top each serving with a spoonful of crust.

Serves 6 to 8 as a first course, or 4 as a main course

GOLDEN STEW OF PUMPKIN, CABBAGE, AND TURMERIC WITH *RISO*

Baking the pumpkin with olive oil and herbs before combining it with the other ingredients gives this stew an added dimension of flavor. *Riso*, Italian pasta shaped like grains of rice, has a delightfully sweet flavor and a slippery texture that I like. If rice is used instead of the *riso*, the soup will have a thicker taste and texture.

Two French pumpkins, Musquée de Provence and Rouge d'Étampes, have bright orange flesh and are ideal for making this colorful stew. Thanks to enterprising market growers, these wonderful pumpkins can sometimes be found at markets in North America. If you can't find them, however, pie-making pumpkin, Sweetmeat squash, and Hubbard squash are good substitutes.

1/2 PUMPKIN, 1/4 HUBBARD SQUASH, OR 1
 SWEETMEAT SQUASH
3 TABLESPOONS OLIVE OIL
1 TABLESPOON GROUND CUMIN
1 TEASPOON GROUND TURMERIC
2 TABLESPOONS DRIED MARJORAM
1/4 CUP WATER (OPTIONAL)
2 TABLESPOONS BUTTER
1 LARGE LEEK, INCLUDING SOME TENDER
 GREEN, CHOPPED
4 CUPS CHICKEN STOCK
1/2 LARGE HEAD CABBAGE, CUT LENGTHWISE
 INTO 1/4-INCH-THICK SLICES
1/4 CUP DRY SHERRY OR DRY WHITE WINE
1/2 CUP COOKED *RISO* PASTA OR WHITE RICE
1 TABLESPOON CHOPPED FRESH CHIVES FOR GARNISH
1 TABLESPOON CHOPPED FRESH TARRAGON
 FOR GARNISH

Preheat an oven to 350°F. Cut the pumpkin or other winter squash into 2-inch squares. You should have about 5 or 6 cups of squares. Leave the skin intact because it is much easier to remove once the squash is baked. Put the squash pieces in a single layer in a flameproof baking dish just large enough to hold them. Sprinkle them with the olive oil, cumin, turmeric, and marjoram. Bake in the preheated oven until tender, about 1 hour. Add the water only if the pieces seem to be in danger of sticking or burning.

Meanwhile, in a saucepan large enough to hold the stew eventually, melt the butter over medium heat and sauté the leek for 2 or 3 minutes. Add the chicken stock and cabbage. Simmer until the cabbage is tender, about 10 minutes. Set aside.

When the squash is done, remove the pieces

Golden Stew of Pumpkin, Cabbage, and Turmeric with Riso

from the baking dish and let them cool slightly. Add the sherry or white wine to the baking dish and cook over medium heat for 3 or 4 minutes, scraping up any browned bits stuck to the pan bottom. Add the resulting pan juices to the chicken stock mixture.

Peel the squash. In a blender or food processor, purée the squash with 1/2 cup of the chicken stock mixture. Repeat the process with the remaining squash. Add the puréed squash to the stock mixture and bring to a boil. Reduce the heat to medium-low and add the cooked *riso* or rice. Simmer for 2 to 3 minutes.

Serve the stew sprinkled with the chives and tarragon.

Serves 6

Freshly Dug Belgian Endive

GRATIN OF BELGIAN ENDIVE

The sweetness of prosciutto and the rich, velvety smoothness of béchamel sauce are perfect counterparts to the slight bitterness of Belgian endive, which is one of my favorite vegetables to grow and cook.

A curious vegetable, Belgian endive is really the end result of two stages of growth, one in the field and the other under forced conditions. In the first stage, the seeds are planted in early summer. They produce a huge, leafy, very bitter plant that looks somewhat like a monstrous hairy spinach. In late fall, stage two begins. The green leafy tops are cut away to within an inch of the crown. The roots of the plant are dug up, buried in a mixture of sand and soil, and kept in a cool, preferably dark place. In about three weeks, stored energy in the roots produces a second growth of leaves that overlap one another, forming torpedo-shaped heads. These are ivory white and very, very tender, with the slight bitterness that I like so much.

Belgian endive leaves are delicious raw in salads, and they mix especially well with winter fruits and nuts. I like them best cooked in this gratin dish. But if I am rushed, I will just toss a few heads, properly called *chicons*, into a pan alongside a roasting chicken and simmer them in the juices.

8 SMALL TO MEDIUM-SIZED HEADS BELGIAN ENDIVE
3 1/2 TABLESPOONS BUTTER
3 TABLESPOONS ALL-PURPOSE FLOUR
1/2 TEASPOON SALT
1/4 TEASPOON FRESHLY GRATED NUTMEG
1/8 TEASPOON CAYENNE PEPPER
1 CUP MILK

1/4 CUP PLUS 1 TABLESPOON FRESHLY GRATED
SWISS CHEESE
4 OUNCES THIN SLICED PROSCIUTTO OR
OTHER AIR-CURED HAM
1/2 TABLESPOON FRESHLY GROUND BLACK PEPPER

Preheat an oven to 375°F. With a small, sharp knife, cut out the inverted V-shaped cores of the Belgian endives with a small, sharp knife. (The core tends to be quite bitter.) Set aside.

To make the sauce, melt the 2 tablespoons of butter in a heavy-bottomed saucepan over medium heat. When the butter begins to foam, remove the pan from the heat and whisk in the flour, salt, nutmeg, and cayenne pepper until a paste forms. Return the pan to medium heat and gradually whisk in the milk in a steady stream. Reduce the heat to low and stir until there are no lumps. Simmer the sauce, stirring occasionally, until it becomes thick enough to coat the back of a spoon, about 10 minutes. Stir in the cheese and continue to cook only until the cheese has melted into the sauce, 2 or 3 minutes. Taste for seasonings and adjust with salt, if necessary.

Using 1/2 tablespoon of the butter, grease the bottom and sides of a shallow ovenproof casserole about 12 to 14 inches long and 8 inches wide, or just large enough to hold the Belgian endives, ham, and sauce. Arrange the Belgian endives in the casserole and top with the ham. Carefully pour the sauce over the top. Cut the remaining 1 tablespoon butter into small bits and dot the surface. Strew the 1 tablespoon grated cheese over the top. Bake in the preheated oven until done, 25 to 30 minutes.

Sprinkle with the black pepper and serve hot.
Serves 4 to 6

HERBED ROULADE WITH GRILLED *RADICCHIO* AND *PANCETTA* FILLING

The smoky, bittersweet taste of grilled *radicchio* is a good match with *pancetta*, which has a smoky, sweet taste of its own. This thin, savory sponge-cake roll is abundantly flavored with fresh sage and thyme. While still warm, two-thirds of the roll is covered with a mixture of chopped *radicchio*, *pancetta*, and a light béchamel sauce. It is then rolled and wrapped snugly in aluminum foil to mold its shape until ready to serve. Although at first the roulade appears complex because of the different steps, it is really quite easy to make.

Gratin of Belgian Endive

Herbed Roulade with Grilled Radicchio *and* Pancetta *Filling*

Savory Sponge Cake

6 EGGS SEPARATED, PLUS 1 WHOLE EGG
1/2 TEASPOON SALT
1/2 CUP ALL-PURPOSE FLOUR
1/4 CUP FINELY CHOPPED FRESH SAGE
2 TABLESPOONS FINELY CHOPPED FRESH THYME

Filling

1 MEDIUM-SIZED TO LARGE HEAD RADICCHIO
2 TABLESPOONS OLIVE OIL
1/2 TEASPOON SALT
1 TEASPOON FINELY CHOPPED FRESH THYME
    LEAVES
1 TEASPOON CRUSHED WHOLE BLACK PEPPERCORNS
2 CUPS WATER
2 OUNCES PANCETTA OR FARM-STYLE BACON,
    FINELY CHOPPED

Béchamel Sauce

2 TABLESPOONS BUTTER
2 TABLESPOONS ALL-PURPOSE FLOUR
1/4 TEASPOON SALT
1/4 TEASPOON PASILLA CHILI POWDER OR
    CAYENNE PEPPER
1 CUP MILK

Line a 10-by-13-by-1-inch jelly-roll pan with waxed paper; do not butter. Preheat an oven to 375°F.

To prepare the cake, beat the egg yolks, salt, and flour together in a large bowl until a stiff paste forms. Add the whole egg and beat again. Place the egg whites in a separate bowl. With a wire whisk or an electric mixer, beat the egg whites until they form very stiff peaks. With the whisk or on low speed with the mixer, beat one fourth of the beaten egg whites into the egg yolk mixture. Gently fold the remaining egg whites, the sage, and thyme into the egg yolk mixture. With a spatula, evenly spread the cake batter in the waxed paper-lined pan, being sure to fill the corners and meet the edges.

Bake the cake in the preheated oven until it is golden but not crisp, 10 to 12 minutes. Remove the cake from the oven and let it cool for 5 or 10 minutes. It will sink and settle a bit.

When it is cool enough to handle, turn the cake out face down onto a piece of aluminum foil that extends at least 1 or 2 inches out on each side of the cake. Carefully peel away the waxed paper. Starting from one of the long edges, roll the cake and foil together lengthwise. This will form the roll before the filling is added. Set the cake aside while you prepare the filling.

To make the filling, slice the *radicchio* into 1/2-inch-wide pieces, cutting from top to stem. In a shallow

Civet *of Rabbit with Pickled Wild Mushrooms and Caper Toasts*

dish, combine the olive oil, salt, peppercorns, and thyme. Add the *radicchio* and marinate for 30 minutes. Meanwhile, prepare a fire in a charcoal grill or preheat a broiler.

Grill or broil the *radicchio* slices for 2 or 3 minutes on each side. They should be slightly browned and crispy on the outside and juicy in the middle. Remove the *radicchio* from the grill or broiler and let cool. Finely chop the *radicchio* and set aside.

In a saucepan bring the water to a boil. Add the *pancetta* or bacon and boil for 5 minutes. Drain and set aside.

To make the sauce, melt the butter in a heavy-bottomed saucepan over medium heat. When the butter begins to foam, remove the pan from the heat and whisk in the flour, salt, and chili powder or cayenne pepper until a paste forms. Return the pan to medium heat and gradually whisk in the milk in a steady stream. Reduce the heat to low and stir until there are

no lumps. Simmer the sauce, stirring occasionally, until it becomes thick enough to coat the back of a spoon, about 10 minutes. Remove from the heat and stir in the *radicchio* and *pancetta*. Let the sauce cool slightly before assembling the roulade.

Unroll the cake so that it lies flat and peel off the aluminum foil. Spread the filling onto two thirds of the surface, leaving an uncovered band along one side the length of the cake. To reroll the cake, lift the filled edge and roll toward the uncovered edge. Gently turn the roll so that the seam is on the bottom.

The roulade is ready to serve. Using a very sharp knife, cut the roll crosswise into 1/2- to 3/4-inch-thick slices. If you prefer to serve the roll piping hot, wrap it in aluminum foil, place it seam side down on a baking sheet, and heat in a preheated 350°F oven for 10 minutes.

Makes 12 to 16 slices; serves 6 to 8

CIVET OF RABBIT WITH PICKLED WILD MUSHROOMS AND CAPER TOASTS

Civet is a traditional French dish made with wild game such as hare or boar. As with bouillabaisse and *soupe au pistou*, there are as many recipes as there are cooks. Generally, the meat is marinated in red wine and regional herbs, sautéed, and then slowly cooked in red wine. The finish—the addition of the blood and the minced liver from the game—accounts for the ensuing rich, dark sauce. It is a wonderful country dish to serve on a cold winter night. Accompanied with bread and wine, a strong cheese, and pears for dessert, the result is a memorable meal.

Since wild game is difficult for most of us to acquire, this *civet* uses domestic rabbit and omits the blood. If your rabbit comes without the liver, substitute a chicken liver. The recipe also calls for pickled mushrooms, which will need to be prepared at least one day in advance of cooking the *civet*.

Because this recipe derives from Provence, juniper berries are included at the insistence of my neighbor, Mme. Delegant. Parisian by origin but married to a Toulonnais, she long ago adopted the regional ingredients of Provence and insists that a truly fine *civet* needs juniper berries.

Marinade
1 CUP DRY RED WINE
1/4 CUP COGNAC
1 TEASPOON SALT
1 TEASPOON FRESHLY GROUND BLACK PEPPER
10 JUNIPER BERRIES, CRUSHED
8 BRANCHES FRESH THYME (EACH 6 TO 8 INCHES LONG), OR 3 TABLESPOONS FRESH THYME LEAVES, MINCED
3 BAY LEAVES
2 BRANCHES FRESH ROSEMARY (EACH 6 TO 8 INCHES LONG), OR 2 TABLESPOONS FRESH ROSEMARY LEAVES, MINCED

1 RABBIT (ABOUT 3 1/2 POUNDS) WITH LIVER, CUT INTO 6 SERVING PIECES
2 OUNCES SALT PORK, BLANCHED 2 MINUTES AND DRAINED
1/4 CUP OLIVE OIL
2 ONIONS, SLICED CROSSWISE INTO 1/2-INCH-THICK ROUNDS
2 CLOVES GARLIC, MINCED
1/4 CUP ALL-PURPOSE FLOUR
1 1/2 BOTTLES DRY RED WINE

Toasts
1/2 CUP (1/4 POUND) BUTTER, SOFTENED
2 TABLESPOONS DRAINED CAPERS
12 SLICES REGULAR FRENCH BREAD (1/2 INCH THICK), OR 24 SMALL BAGUETTE SLICES
1/2 CUP PICKLED WILD MUSHROOMS (PAGE 134)

In a glass or ceramic bowl, combine all of the ingredients for the marinade. Add the rabbit pieces (reserve the liver) to the marinade and turn them to coat them well. Marinate for several hours at room temperature.

When you are ready to make the stew, remove the rabbit pieces from the marinade and reserve the marinade. Dry the pieces thoroughly. Cut the salt pork into 1/2-inch cubes. Place the cubes in a dutch oven or a large flameproof casserole and cook for 10 to 15 minutes over low heat to melt the fat. Add the olive oil and onions. Sauté the onions over medium heat until translucent, about 5 minutes. Add the garlic and rabbit pieces and cook over medium heat, turning the rabbit pieces, until lightly browned, 10 to 15 minutes. Remove the rabbit pieces from the pan and set aside.

Add the flour to the pan and stir constantly over medium heat for 4 to 5 minutes until a brown roux forms. Very slowly whisk 1/2 bottle of the red wine into the roux. Continue whisking as the sauce begins to thicken. Return the rabbit pieces to the pan and turn them to coat them with the sauce. Add the remaining wine and turn the rabbit some more.

If you used whole herbs in the marinade, gather the thyme and rosemary branches and bay leaves from the marinade, tie them in a bouquet garni, and add the bouquet garni to the pan, along with the juniper berries. Cover and cook slowly over low heat until the rabbit is just tender, 45 minutes to 1 hour. Remove the rabbit pieces from the pan and keep warm.

Remove the bouquet garni if you used one. Strain the sauce into a saucepan. Place the sauce over low heat, taste, and correct the seasonings. Reduce the sauce, if necessary, to thicken it.

Meanwhile, in a food processor or blender, purée the raw liver until it is very smooth. Strain the liver, if necessary, to remove any sinews. Set the liver aside.

Preheat the broiler. To make the toasts, in a small bowl cream together the butter and capers until they form a smooth, spreadable paste. Spread each bread slice with some of the flavored butter and arrange them on a broiler pan.

Remove the sauce from the fire, stir in the puréed liver and the pickled mushrooms, and return the pan to low heat to cook for only 1 minute, just to warm the liver and the mushrooms. It is very important not to overcook the liver. Return the rabbit to the pan to warm it gently. At the same time slip the buttered bread slices into the broiler and broil 2 or 3 minutes until just barely golden.

Serve the *civet* on individual plates with the hot toasts garnishing each plate.

Ingredients for **Civet** *of Rabbit*

Serves 4

FRENCH SHEPHERD'S PIE WITH CELERY ROOT AND POTATO TOPPING

Shepherd's pie, a traditional English dish, is meat stew covered with a thick layer of mashed potatoes and then lightly browned in the oven. In this version the topping is a combination of mashed potatoes and pungent celery root.

Celery root has a somewhat intimidating appearance. It is not at all obvious to the uninitiated how it is used in the kitchen. When I was a student in Aix-en-Provence, my French roommate taught me that once the whorled and callused skin of the celery root was removed, the flesh could be cooked or eaten raw in any number of different ways. An inexpensive winter root, its strong flavor and interesting texture made it frequent fare in our kitchen and also in the inexpensive restaurants we frequented, where it most often appeared as *céleri-rave rémoulade*.

4 TABLESPOONS BUTTER

1 1/2 TO 2 POUNDS BONELESS LAMB STEW MEAT,
 CUT INTO 1-INCH PIECES

3 FRESH BAY LEAVES, OR 1 DRIED BAY LEAF

1 1/2 TEASPOONS SALT

1 1/2 TEASPOONS FRESHLY GROUND BLACK PEPPER

1 TABLESPOON ALL-PURPOSE FLOUR

1 CUP BEEF STOCK

4 POTATOES, PEELED AND QUARTERED

2 MEDIUM-SIZED OR 1 LARGE CELERY ROOT,
 PEELED AND CUT INTO 1-INCH CUBES
 (SEE NOTE)

1/4 CUP MILK

1 EGG

1 TEASPOON CHOPPED FRESH THYME

Melt 1 tablespoon of the butter in a large skillet over medium-high heat. Add the lamb and brown lightly on all sides, about 10 minutes. Add the bay leaves, sprinkle with 1 teaspoon each of the salt and pepper and the flour, and continue to cook, stirring constantly. The flour will start to brown on the bottom of the pan, but don't let it burn. Let it become very dark brown, as it is the browning flour that will eventually give the stew its rich, dark color. This will take 6 to 8 minutes. Stirring the meat and scraping the pan bottom, add the stock, a little at a time, until all the bits of browned flour are freed from the pan bottom and mixed into the

French Shepherd's Pie with Celery Root and Potato Topping

liquid. Cover the pan, reduce the heat, and simmer until the lamb is very tender and separates with a fork, 1 1/2 to 2 hours. The cooking time may vary because the age of meat sold as lamb ranges considerably from very young to almost a yearling.

While the lamb is cooking, boil the potatoes in water to cover until tender, about 30 minutes. At the same time, in a separate pan boil the celery root in water to cover. The celery root will take a little less time to cook—only 15 to 20 minutes—than the potatoes.

Drain the potatoes, reserving 1/4 cup of their cooking water, and place them in a bowl. Drain the celery root and set aside 1 cup of the cubes to add to the stew. Add the remaining cubes to the potatoes and mash them together. Add the reserved potato cooking water, the milk, 2 tablespoons of the butter, egg, the remaining 1/2 teaspoon each salt and pepper, and the thyme. Whisk all the ingredients until well blended and fairly smooth.

Preheat an oven to 375°F. To assemble the pie, put the stew in an ovenproof casserole and stir in the reserved celery root cubes. Spoon the potato mixture evenly over the top to cover completely. Cut the remaining 1 tablespoon butter into bits and dot the potato topping with the bits.

Place the casserole in the preheated oven until the topping is lightly browned and the stew is bubbling, 15 to 20 minutes.

Serves 4 to 6

Note: Once it is exposed to the air, cut celery root discolors. If you are not going to use the celery root immediately, put the cubes into a bowl of cold water to cover and add 1/4 cup vinegar or fresh lemon juice to prevent discoloration.

POPOVERS FILLED WITH BEEF AND LEEK STEW

Leeks have a characteristic sweetness that sets them apart from the other commonly used members of the *Allium*, or onion, family. They are often added to stocks and stews because of the sweet flavor they impart.

In this dish, the natural sweetness of the leeks is enhanced and intensified when the pan is deglazed with balsamic vinegar and the stew is simmered until the leeks have melted into a rich brown sauce. The meat becomes so tender that it is easily shredded with a fork. The robust stew is then spooned into a bed of popovers fresh from the oven and topped with slices of steamed leeks.

3 LARGE LEEKS
2 TABLESPOONS OLIVE OIL
1 1/2 TO 2 POUNDS BONELESS BEEF CHUCK ROAST, CUT INTO 2-INCH CHUNKS
2 TABLESPOONS ALL-PURPOSE FLOUR
1 TEASPOON SALT
1/2 TEASPOON FRESHLY GROUND BLACK PEPPER
1/4 CUP BALSAMIC VINEGAR
3 TO 4 CUPS WATER

Popovers
1 1/4 CUPS ALL-PURPOSE FLOUR
1/2 TEASPOON SALT
1/2 TEASPOON SUGAR
1 CUP MILK
1 TABLESPOON BUTTER, MELTED
2 EGGS
VEGETABLE OIL OR MELTED BUTTER FOR MUFFIN TIN

Popovers Filled with Beef and Leek Stew

Cut the leeks in half lengthwise, then cut them crosswise into 1/2-inch-thick slices. Include all but the final 2 or 3 inches of the green shaft.

Heat the olive oil in a heavy-bottomed flame-proof casserole or skillet over medium-high heat. Add the beef and cook until browned, 8 to 10 minutes. Add all but 1/2 cup of the leeks to the beef and cook for 4 or 5 minutes, stirring often. Sprinkle the leeks and beef with the flour, salt, and pepper and cook for another 3 or 4 minutes to brown the flour. Add the balsamic vinegar and deglaze the pan, scraping up any browned bits that cling to the bottom. Slowly add 2 cups of the water and bring to a boil, continuing to stir. Reduce the heat and cover the pan. Simmer the stew until a thick sauce has formed and the meat can be cut with a fork, about 2 hours. Add additional water, a little at a time, as needed to keep the meat moist.

Start to make the popovers about 1 hour before the stew will be done. Preheat an oven to 475°F.

Combine the flour, salt, sugar, milk, 1 tablespoon melted butter, and eggs in a bowl and beat with a whisk or electric mixer until thoroughly blended, 2 to 3 minutes. Brush a 12-cup muffin tin with a little oil or butter and heat it in the preheated oven for a few minutes. Fill each muffin cup one half to three fourths full with the batter.

Bake the popovers in the preheated oven for 15 minutes. Reduce the heat to 350°F and bake until they are deeply browned and puffed, about 20 minutes.

While the popovers are baking, arrange the reserved 1/2 cup leeks on a steamer rack over gently boiling water. Cover and steam until the leeks are limp but still retain their color, 4 or 5 minutes.

To serve, place 2 popovers on each warmed plate. Break open the popovers and spoon the stew over them. Top with the steamed leeks.

Serves 6

Oven-Roasted Chips of Winter Roots

Celery root, parsnip, rutabaga, turnip, and fennel all have distinctly different tastes and textures. Roasting brings out the flavor of each, and using them in combination is a simple way to bring a wide range of tastes to the plate. Parsnips are dense, rich, and sweet, while celery roots are full of the sharp, pungent taste of home-grown celery. Dark orange rutabagas have a strong taste of the earth, and turnips possess a faint mustard taste. Licorice-flavored fennel isn't a proper root at all, but it fits right in with the other roots in this recipe. Use this mix of roots to accompany roasts and chops as a change from roasted potatoes.

2 PARSNIPS

1 LARGE TURNIP

1 LARGE RUTABAGA

1 LARGE OR 2 MEDIUM-SIZED FENNEL BULBS

1 CELERY ROOT

2 TO 3 TABLESPOONS OLIVE OIL

1 TEASPOON SALT

1/2 TEASPOON FRESHLY GROUND BLACK PEPPER

Preheat an oven to 475°F. Trim the parsnips and peel them. Cut them lengthwise into 1/4-inch-thick slices. Peel the turnip and the rutabaga. Cut each of them into quarters and then into 1/4-inch-thick slices. Trim away the top of the fennel bulb(s) and remove any brown or tough outer layers. Cut the bulb(s) in half lengthwise and then into slices 1/4 inch thick. Peel the celery root and cut it in the same manner as the fennel.

Put all of the vegetables in a bowl with the olive oil. Toss the vegetables to coat them lightly with the oil. Season with the salt and pepper. Spread the vegetables evenly on a baking sheet large enough to hold them in a single layer.

Roast the vegetables in the preheated oven for 8 to 10 minutes. Turn the vegetable slices and cook until slightly crisped and tender, 5 to 7 minutes longer.

Serve very hot.

Serves 4 to 6

Oven-Roasted Chips of Winter Roots

Wild Mushrooms for Pickling

PICKLED WILD MUSHROOMS

In France meaty *sanguins* (*Lactaryus delicious*) are eagerly hunted beneath the pine trees of Provence in fall. In plentiful mushroom years, any *sanguins* not grilled immediately with garlic and olive oil or sautéed with eggs are pickled for later use. The readily available *shiitake* mushrooms are a good substitute for *sanguins*

because they are meaty enough to stand up to pickling and, like *sanguins*, have a distinct flavor of their own that is enhanced, not overwhelmed, by pickling.

Serve these pickled mushrooms as a condiment or use them as an ingredient in dishes such as *Civet of Rabbit with Pickled Wild Mushrooms and Caper Toasts* (page 127).

Pickling Mixture
1/2 CUP OLIVE OIL
ABOUT 1/2 CUP RED WINE VINEGAR
3/4 TEASPOON SALT
1/2 TEASPOON WHOLE BLACK PEPPERCORNS
4 SPRIGS FRESH THYME

4 OUNCES *SANGUIN* OR *SHIITAKE* MUSHROOMS,
QUARTERED (ABOUT 2 CUPS)

To make the pickling mixture, combine 1/4 cup of the olive oil, 1/4 cup of the vinegar, 1/2 teaspoon of the salt, the peppercorns, and thyme in a medium-sized saucepan. Bring to a boil over medium heat and boil for 2 minutes. Reduce the heat to very low, add the mushrooms, and cook for 2 minutes more, turning the mushrooms constantly.

Put the mushrooms and the olive oil mixture into a clean pint jar. Add the remaining 1/4 cup olive oil and 1/4 teaspoon salt, plus enough of the remaining vinegar to cover the mushrooms. Cover the jar loosely with aluminum foil and let it cool to room temperature. Put the lid on the jar and refrigerate.

Within 24 hours the mushrooms will have absorbed the flavors of the pickling mixture. These will keep up to 1 month in the refrigerator.

Makes about 1 pint

SORBET OF ARMAGNAC-
PRESERVED CHERRIES

I feel intensely rewarded by my spring condiment making when I prepare this sorbet. I keep the preserved cherries in the back of the refrigerator throughout the summer and fall, waiting for that special occasion when I will bring the ice-cream maker up from the basement and make the beautiful pale garnet-colored sorbet that has become my choice of winter dessert. The resulting ice is sweet, dotted with small Armagnac-soaked cherries. After adding a garnish of a whole cherry or two and a scant spoonful of the Armagnac, the balance of sweet and tart seems near perfect.

Sorbet of Armagnac-Preserved Cherries

If you haven't preserved cherries or other fruits, such as plums, they may be purchased at specialty stores. You may well find that they are preserved not in Armagnac, but in Marc de Bourgogne or another liquor. Generally speaking, fruits in France will be preserved in the liquor produced in the region. In southwest France, Armagnac is used; in Burgundy, Marc de Bourgogne is the choice. Historically, members of France's wine cooperatives had the right to a certain number of liters of *eau-de-vie*, or the distilled product of the grape skins, stems, and seeds, and that was the liquor most commonly used in Provence for preserving fruits and for making homemade fortified wines for aperitifs. The generation that came of age during World War I was the last to have that right, however. Since few from that era are left, the *eau-de-vie* must now be purchased.

Today a variety of liquors are used for preserving, among them Armagnac. I like the strong, slightly burnt flavor it imparts to cherries and plums. To preserve cherries or plums yourself, choose very perfect, ripe fruits. Leave the stems on the cherries. They make pretty garnishes that way. Wash and dry the fruits carefully and put them into clean jars that have been rinsed with boiling water. Cover them with the best Armagnac or other brandy that you can afford. Store them in the refrigerator. They will be ready to eat in about a month and will last indefinitely, although they will become quite strong after a year or so.

1/3 CUP PLUS 6 TO 8 TEASPOONS ARMAGNAC
      FROM THE PRESERVED CHERRIES
3 CUPS WATER
1 1/2 CUPS SUGAR
JUICE OF 1/2 LEMON

1/2 CUP ARMAGNAC-PRESERVED CHERRIES,
PITTED AND COARSELY CHOPPED
12 ARMAGNAC-PRESERVED CHERRIES FOR GARNISH

Combine 1/3 cup Armagnac from the preserved cherries, the water, and sugar in a small saucepan. Bring to a boil, stirring to dissolve the sugar. Boil for 5 minutes to form a light syrup. Remove from the heat and let cool to room temperature. Stir in the lemon juice.

Following the manufacturer's directions, freeze the syrup in an ice-cream maker, or freeze in ice-cube trays in the freezer. When frozen stir in the chopped, pitted cherries and pack the sorbet into a bowl or other container. Place in the freezer for several hours before serving.

When ready to serve, spoon a teaspoon or so of the Armagnac from the preserved cherries onto each individual serving plate or bowl. Add 1 or 2 scoops of the sorbet and garnish with the reserved cherries.

Makes 1 quart sorbet; serves 6 to 8

TARTE TATIN OF QUINCES AND GOLDEN RAISINS

In France wild and abandoned quince trees border country roads, a *potager* may have a quince tree or two at its edge, and the fruits are regularly found in open markets during fall and early winter. Quinces remain popular in France, unlike in the United States where they have practically disappeared from the market and where the fruits of old trees are left ungathered.

Quinces, unpalatable when raw, are transformed by cooking. Their color turns from starchy white to pale gold or deep amber, depending upon variety, and the flavor that develops is slightly musky, with an underlying hint of citrus. Quinces have little natural sugar, so sugar is generally added.

In this dish, sliced quinces absorb the colors and tastes of a sugary wine marinade. When cooked, the fruit softens beneath the crust and a wonderful caramel syrup forms from the butter, sugar, and juices.

This *tarte tatin* is delicious served plain or with heavy cream or ice cream.

6 RIPE LARGE OR 8 SMALL YELLOW QUINCES
(ABOUT 4 POUNDS; SEE NOTE)
2 CUPS MERLOT WINE
1/2 CUP SUGAR
1 PIECE VANILLA BEAN (ABOUT 2 INCHES LONG)
1 CUP GOLDEN RAISINS

Pastry Dough
2 CUPS ALL-PURPOSE FLOUR
1 TEASPOON SALT
1/2 CUP (1/4 POUND) UNSALTED BUTTER, CHILLED
3 TABLESPOONS MARGARINE, CHILLED
6 TABLESPOONS ICE WATER

2 TABLESPOONS BUTTER
1/2 CUP SUGAR

Peel and core the quinces and cut them into slices about 3/8 inch thick. Place them in a bowl with the wine, sugar, vanilla bean, and raisins. Cover and let stand at room temperature overnight.

Tarte Tatin of Quinces and Golden Raisins

To make the pastry dough, sift the flour and salt together in a bowl. Cut the butter and margarine into 1/2-inch chunks and add them to the flour mixture. With a pastry blender or 2 knives, cut in the butter and margarine until pea-sized balls form. Add the ice water, 1 tablespoon at a time. As you add the water, turn the dough lightly with a fork and then with your fingertips. This will help to keep the pastry light and flaky. Do not overwork the dough or it will become tough. Gather the dough into a ball, wrap in plastic wrap or aluminum foil, and refrigerate it for 15 minutes. It will be easier to roll out if it is chilled.

Using 1 tablespoon of the butter, heavily butter a baking dish 9 or 10 inches in diameter and 2 to 2 1/2 inches deep. Sprinkle the bottom of the buttered dish with 1/4 cup of the sugar. With a slotted utensil remove the quince slices and raisins from the wine marinade. Arrange the quince slices in a layer on the bottom of the baking dish. Add one-third of the raisins and one-third of the remaining sugar. Repeat the process twice. Cut the remaining 1 tablespoon butter into small bits and dot the top. Preheat the oven to 375°F.

On a lightly floured board, roll out the pastry dough 1/8 inch thick and about the same diameter as the baking dish. Drape it around the rolling pin and transfer it to the baking dish. Unfold it and gently place it over the quince, allowing it to droop inside the dish. Press the edge of the crust against the dish sides. Prick the top with the tines of a fork. Bake in the preheated oven for 45 minutes to 1 hour. You can tell when the tart is done because a thick, dark, garnet-colored syrup will have formed in the bottom of the dish.

This is an upside-down pie, so when it is done, you must immediately unmold it. Invert a serving platter on top of the baking dish and, holding the platter and baking dish firmly, flip them. Serve warm.

Serves 6 to 8

Note: If quince are unavailable, 4 pounds winter pears or tart apples such as Granny Smiths may be substituted.

If you wish to caramelize the top of the finished tart even more, unmold the tart onto a flameproof platter, sprinkle it with 1 tablespoon sugar, and slip it into a preheated broiler for 2 to 3 minutes.

A Simple *Potager* Plan
for a Small Space

Since the purpose of the *potager* is to furnish the kitchen with fresh vegetables throughout the year, the size of the garden will depend upon time, space, inclination, and need.

Once you have decided that you want a kitchen garden and that you have the basic elements necessary for one—sun, water, and either gardening ground or a place for containers—the choices of what to plant, where, and of how much space to devote to the garden are mostly personal. A classic *potager* contains herbs, annual vegetables, and a few cutting flowers. Ideally it also has a few perennials such as asparagus, artichokes, and strawberries. If you have more space, then grapevines and one or two favorite fruit or nut trees can be planted at the edge. Dwarf trees of most fruit and nut varieties are available, and fit nicely into a small garden scheme. In "modern" *potagers* in France, it is not uncommon to find an espaliered dwarf apple tree or two between rows of vegetables. This is a break with the classic *potager* that allows only berry fruits, not tree fruits, in the garden proper. I find it an appealing concept to have a dwarf tree or two in the garden, especially since today most of us have limited space—and time—for gardening.

This simple nine-by-twelve-foot seasonal *potager* plan includes herbs, salad greens, potatoes, summer vegetables, and fall pumpkins. The garden can be started anytime of the year that the ground can be worked; in other words, work can begin when the earth is not frozen and when it will be at least two months before a hard frost. A *potager* can be launched in spring with a first planting of peas, lettuces, carrots, and potatoes. It can be started in early summer with green bean seeds, tomato and pepper seedlings, summer squashes, pumpkins, and some zinnias. In late summer the garden can be planted with lettuces, leeks, radishes, and turnips.

Preparing the Garden Site

Regardless of which season you choose to start your garden, plan on allowing a period in which to free your garden site from currently growing weeds. You must also allot time for the weed seeds to germinate in the soil so that you can remove them. The latter is very important, for if you plant your garden with vegetable and flower seeds without first ridding it of existing weed seeds, your seeds and the weed seeds will germinate at the same time. Then you will have a great deal of work freeing the tiny vegetable and flower seedlings that are intermixed with the weed seedlings. I have learned this the hard way, watching my beautiful rows of delicate lettuces being taken over by rapidly growing cheese weeds, pig weeds, and wild grasses, and have saved them only by aggressive and repeated hoeing.

If the ground is soft enough, turn it over with a shovel or a powered tiller to a depth of a foot or so.

Smooth the ground, breaking down any big clods and pulling out any weeds that are too large to turn over easily into the earth. Rake the site level and divide it into twelve squares each *roughly* three feet on a side. The plot should be three squares wide at the top and bottom and four squares on a side. Plan on running two paths, each about a foot wide, between the rows down the length of the plot. These paths will allow you to reach all the parts of the garden without stepping on any plants.

Don't plant the garden now, no matter how much you want to begin. Instead, water it and watch for more weed seeds to sprout. When the weed seedlings are less than two inches high, hoe them again, cutting their roots and cultivating the soil. Rake again, this time mounding the soil of each square into a level bed about six inches high. Now you are ready to plant.

PLANTING THE GARDEN

The ground is ideal for planting when the weeds have just been removed and the soil is moist just below the surface. Scratch down through the top inch of the soil to where it is damp, and then plant your seeds deep into this moist layer. Press the soil firmly back over the seeds to retain the moisture. There should be enough dampness to germinate the seeds but not so much that the weed seeds will start again until you water the garden in a week or so. By the time more weeds grow, your seedlings will have a good, strong start.

Alternatively, plant your seeds in the ground two or three days after you have cut down the second crop of weeds and water them immediately. Your seeds will still have a head start over the weeds and your garden will be underway.

The *potager* is a rotational garden that is in an almost constant state of being seeded, cultivated, and harvested. While one season's harvest is in progress, another cleared garden space is being planted with the next season's seeds. The lists below characterize the vegetables that are best planted during a particular season. Those that are starred are the easiest to grow.

SPRING

Spring vegetables need cool weather and water to grow and remain tender. When the days become hot, the leaf vegetables become tough and the root vegetables become pithy and fibrous.

In early spring plant:
Arugula*, Carrots*, Chervil*, Chives*, Dandelion*, Leeks, Lettuce*, Peas*, Radishes*, Nasturtiums*, Sweet peas*

In late spring plant:
Beets, Pattypan squashes*, Zucchini*

SUMMER

In summer plants produce leafy or vining growths, but we eat the fruiting bodies. To produce mature fruits, plants need warm soil and warm temperatures, along with adequate water.

In early summer plant:
Basil*, Dill, Eggplants, Melons, Parsley, Shell beans*, Snap beans*, Sweet peppers

In mid-summer plant:
Fennel, Leeks, Pumpkins, *Radicchio**, Bachelor buttons, Cosmos, Sunflowers, Zinnias

FALL

The fall garden is actually planted in late summer with seeds very much like those of spring. Fall vegetables are leafy greens and young roots, some of which will be harvested quickly and others that will stay in place over winter, depending upon the severity of the climate.

In late summer or early fall plant:
Arugula*, Chard, Escarole*, *Frisée**, Green chicories*, Lettuce*, Radishes*, Spinach, Turnips*

Plant each of the garden squares with seeds appropriate for the season, choosing from the above lists. As you harvest one season's crop—radishes, for example—plant your garden square with seeds for the next season.

Many herbs are difficult to grow from seeds, especially the perennials, which grow year after year

and are best planted as seedlings or cuttings. Buy the perennial herbs listed below in small pots or flats from a garden center and transplant them into the garden anytime of the year.

Marjoram, Mint, Oregano, Rosemary, Sage, Sorrel, Summer savory, Tarragon, Thyme, Winter savory

Other herbs are readily grown from seed, particularly annuals, that is, those that must be resown every year. Below are the most common culinary herbs to grow from seed.

Arugula, Basil, Chervil, Chives, Dill, Parsley

PERENNIALS, BULBS, AND TUBERS

If you want to plant perennials—asparagus, artichokes, strawberries—consult your local garden center for the best varieties for your area and for the best time of the year to plant them.

Potatoes, onions, and garlic are all easy to grow, if you have the space. Plant them along the edges of your squares, or fill a square or two with these instead of with seasonal seeds.

And, finally, don't be afraid to fail. Prepare the soil, plant the seeds, water the garden, and nature will take care of almost everything else except the weeding. Remember, don't be discouraged if something doesn't grow. All gardeners fail with a plant or a seed or a garden scheme, usually several times each season.

Enjoy the *potager* for what it is—a daily source of fresh vegetables and herbs grown by you for your kitchen.

Potager

INDEX

Index

Index

To My Family and Friends

G.B.

To Robert Steffy and Donna Warner

J.V.

ACKNOWLEDGMENTS

We would like to extend our thanks to the following:

First of all, a very special and heartfelt thank you to Bill Goldsmith whose beautiful garden is the introductory photo of the book and whose inviting open doorway appears on the cover. His home, his tableware, and his artistic and culinary skills, all of which he so generously shared, were an inspiration to us. We appreciate too, the wise supervision his cat, Fred, provided for our activities.

The people who so graciously lent us their homes, kitchens, and gardens to photograph and who were always at hand to step in and help with flower arranging, soup stirring, or other sundry tasks.

In California: Alta Tingle, Mimi Luebbermann, Lisbeth and John Farmar-Bowers, and the Wetzel family. In France: Bill Goldsmith, Joanne Kaufmann, William and Lynn McKee, Patricia and Walter Wells, Georgina and Denys Fine, M and Mme Michaud, M and Mme Marcel Palazolli, Mme Nathalie Waag, and Claude Brissemoret, who let us photograph in his Paris restaurant, Brissemoret.

The food stylists and cooks whose ideas, help, suggestions, and enthusiasms are all part of this book.

In California, Karen Frerichs and Patricia Curtan, and in France: Adele and Pascal Degremont, Vania and Isabel Fine, Johann and Muriel Fine, and Bill Goldsmith.

The farmers and gardeners who gave us all the fruits, vegetables, and flowers we asked for, and more.

In California: Stonefree Farm in Davis, Terry Schroeder in Winters, and California Specialties in Dixon. In France: M and Mme Marcel Palazolli and M and Mme Robert Lamy.

The Gardener in Berkeley and Lucia Jahsman Pottery Studio in Sonoma, California; JMV Fine Atelier in Moustiers-Ste.-Marie, France; and Site-Corot/The Bill Goldsmith Collection, Limoges, France and New York, for beautiful and very special tableware.

The Alexander Valley Winery near Healdsburg, California, for providing their wines and the fruits of their garden and orchards.

The Sonoma Flower Company in Santa Rosa, California, for providing us with their glorious garden roses and field flowers.

And our special thanks to Nathalie Waag of Bonnieux, France, for taking time from her "A Week in Provence" clients to escort us through the market in Apt, France, and to introduce us to her favorite market vendors and their wares.

And thank you to Maria Gresham for all her support and help in getting this project off the ground.

Georgeanne Brennan
John Vaughan